HITTING THE MARK

ASSESSMENT TOOLS FOR TEACHERS

Don Aker

Pembroke Publishers Limited

To
Deborah Aker
best critic, best friend
and to
teachers everywhere
who are students first and always

© 1995 Pembroke Publishers Limited
538 Hood Road
Markham, Ontario L3R 3K9

Canadian Cataloguing in Publication Data

Aker, Don, 1955-
  Hitting the mark

ISBN 1-55138-062-5

1. Grading and marking (Students). I. Title.

LB3051.A54 1995   373.12'7   C95-931608-6

A catalogue record for this book is available from the British
Library.
Published in the U.K. by
Drake Educational Associates
St. Fagan's Road, Fairwater, Cardiff CF5 3AE

Editor: David Kilgour
Design: John Zehethofer
Cover Photography: Ajay Photographics
Typesetting: Jay Tee Graphics Ltd.

Printed and bound in Canada
9 8 7 6 5 4 3 2 1

Table of Contents

Foreword: The Education Cookbook

"Neither a borrower nor a lender be."
Polonius in *Hamlet, Prince of Demark* (Act I, Scene iii),
by William Shakespeare

Although written four hundred years ago, Polonius's instruction to his son, Laertes, is sound advice indeed. In fact, considering current economic trends, most modern parents might extend the same counsel to their own children — I, for instance, need look no further than last month's Visa statement to remind myself of the importance of Polonius's words.

Polonius's advice, however, has absolutely no place in education. Good teachers are borrowers *and* lenders, people who seek out and willingly share instructional strategies, creative assignments, motivational ideas, record-keeping tips, anything and everything that can help make learning more meaningful and teaching more manageable. Ask a group of teachers to assess the effectiveness of an in-service presentation or professional conference and I'll wager most will do so according to the number of practical ideas or strategies they've acquired which they can apply to their own teaching situations.

Yes, good teachers are borrowers and lenders. Implicit in this view of educators, however, is an assumption that needs addressing: that good teaching is the result of finding the best ideas, the best strategies, the best assignments and making them one's own. It's an assumption that needs addressing because it simply is not true. I know this because I made the same assumption and, unfortunately, it shaped much of my early teaching. I spent years poring over methodology texts and attending in-services looking for the best ideas/strategies/ assignments, experiencing along the way numerous epiphanies as I concluded that, finally, *this* time I'd found the answer to the problem of teaching whatever a particular curriculum dictated. I was a "cookbook educator," confident that if I had all the ingredients and followed the recipe perfectly I could achieve with my students the same results as those teachers whose efforts I emulated. Often, though, I was disappointed with the results I saw, never entirely sure what I'd done wrong.

I recall vividly, for example, the first time I encountered teacher/author Nancie Atwell and her workshop approach to teaching reading and writing. Speaking at a teachers' conference, Atwell described how she and her grade eight students wrote literary letters to each other about the books they read, and I sat spellbound as she shared letters by adolescents who had connected with literature on both a personal and a critical level. I left that conference convinced I'd at last found the strategy for teaching literature I'd been looking for, and I spent the following months trying to evoke in my students the same responses Atwell had elicited from hers.

While I experienced some success with my senior classes, my eighth-graders wrote letters to me and each other which seldom contained more than perfunctory comments about plot and vague recommendations (or non-recommendations) that others read a particular book. Despite my prodding them to include personal connections with the literature they were reading and to reflect on some of the decisions the authors of that literature had made, they continued to write comments like "It's a good book. You'd like it. Everybody dies." By Christmas I had abandoned literary letters with this grade level.

A year later, I stumbled across an article written by a junior high teacher who had tried Atwell's approach with her grade sevens, and in it she included copies of letters that were very much like the ones I had received from my grade eights. Much to my surprise, however, she identified how the letters demonstrated real growth in her students' perception of the literature they were reading. Comparing letters written at the beginning of the school year with those written by the same students the following spring, she showed how her students had begun to question and, in some cases, harshly criticize the choices authors had made in the stories, poems, and novels they had written.

I was stunned. Had Atwell's strategy been working all along

with my grade eights? Why hadn't I recognized it when this teacher obviously had? Part of the answer lay in the fact that I'd given up on literary letters too soon, but that was only a small part of it. Staring at that article, I knew there was a much more important reason: I had expected my students to perform in a specific manner — to write letters like those Atwell's students had written — and I hadn't been ready to view other results as valid indicators that learning was indeed occurring.

It was at that moment that I experienced the real epiphany which has guided my teaching from that day to this: the problem with focusing on strategies is that teachers sometimes use them with little consideration about expected outcomes. Too often, questions like "What will I teach?" and "What is the best way to teach this?" occupy all of a teacher's attention at the expense of more crucial concerns: "Why am I using this?" "What learning do I hope it will encourage?" "How will my students demonstrate what they have learned?" Most important, however, is the question "How do kids learn?"

I am embarrassed to admit that my initial teacher-training placed little emphasis on learning theory. Yes, my classmates and I looked at Piaget and, of course, Maslow's hierarchy of needs, but as secondary-teachers-in-training we paid little attention to concerns not directly related to methodology and classroom management. (We thought the "Don't smile until Christmas" credo was the single most important lesson we'd learned.) What is even more embarrassing to admit is that I taught high school language arts for several years without understanding how kids learn to read in the first place.

I am grateful to my children for so many things: for showing me the beauty in pavement rainbows where previously I saw only oil spills, for reminding me of the mystery of snowflake uniqueness, for helping me see through new eyes everything I once took for granted. And for showing me how kids learn. That article written by the grade seven teacher might not have had such an impact on me had it not been for my children — I read it at a time when my daughters were respectively two years old and a few months old and I was witness to learning in a way I'd never perceived it in my classroom. My entire perception of the way children make meaning of the world around them was ripening, and I began to recognize the importance of learning theory and its implications for what I did in my classroom.

Having witnessed my daughters' learning and having subsequently explored learning theory through research and personal reading and writing, I have much to say now about how kids learn that I couldn't say before. I know that knowledge isn't something a student can be given, that students learn by *doing*, by being actively involved in the process. I know that students need to use language to learn, to talk ideas through until those ideas become their own. I know that students must have the opportunity to experiment and to approximate in their learning, and that I must respect and value their early efforts — however rudimentary — to draw meaning from the experiences they encounter.

When I judged Atwell's letter-writing strategy a failure with my eighth-graders, I did so because I failed to understand what my students' learning would look like. On the other hand, when my daughters took their first faltering steps and collapsed on the carpet, I didn't berate them for falling because I *knew* they would fall; I celebrated their efforts with praise and hugs and kisses. As teachers, we need to celebrate the stumbling efforts of our students as they try to make sense of what we want them to learn. We cannot do this, however, by being only borrowers and lenders, cookbook educators who focus on the "how" of teaching and concern ourselves more with strategies than with the outcomes those strategies make possible.

The purpose of this book is to offer teachers at the secondary level suggestions and guidelines for assessment within a framework which reflects current learning theory. It is not a collection of recipes. It is my attempt to help teachers ensure and demonstrate accountability to their students, to parents, to administrators, and, most of all, to themselves.

1 / The Language of Assessment

"What are you going to give him?" the young man asked. He was very tall and his long legs bent at acute angles between the chair and the coffee table.

The young woman sitting across from him sighed. "I don't know," she said, sifting through a sheaf of papers in a worn folder. "The illustrations are fantastic, but there's not much writing." She paused as she came to one picture and held it out in front of her. It was a dramatic sketch of an old man drawn with a minimum of thick, dark lines. "I didn't even ask them to include artwork." She slid it back into the folder and set it on her lap, shaking her head.

The young man nodded sympathetically. "I know what you mean," he said, pulling a duotang from a knapsack under his chair. "I'm trying to decide what to do with all these." He passed the duotang to her and she opened it, revealing class lists with several columns filled with numbers. "I've got eight or nine marks for every student," said the young man. "I'm supposed to make up a single mark for everyone by Thursday to hand in before we go. Any ideas?"

The woman glanced through the lists. "What're these marks for?" she asked, pointing to the last column.

"That was their final test. I was going to make that worth half of the whole unit, but they didn't do very well, did they?" He ran a hand through his hair. "I was thinking that since they spent so long on the project, maybe I could make it worth the most," his last comment sounding more like a question than a statement.

Sitting at a rectangular table by the window, I was the only other person in the staffroom. A stack of assignments and my record book lay sprawled in front of me as I leaned back and sipped my cold coffee. Although the faces were different, the scene before me was one I'd seen several times before: student-teachers nearing the end of their practicum now facing the task of arriving at an overall assessment of their students' performance during the period they had taught at our school.

Listening to them — and others before and after them — discuss the problem of assigning marks that would reflect not only the relative weights of the tests and assignments students had completed but also the learning processes the students had involved themselves in, I recalled the years I had agonized over it. The undergraduate courses I had taken at university had not prepared me for the very real problem at the secondary level of reducing a student's term work (which included myriad anecdotal comments as well as numerous marks for assignments, presentations, quizzes, tests, and an examination) to a single percentage which could be recorded on a report card. After all, this percentage is supposed to mean something. Unfortunately, what it often suggests is far different than the everyday reality of teaching and learning. What teacher, for example, has not grimaced over awarding a 90% to a student who contributed very little to class discussions, submitted lacklustre assignments, yet wrote an excellent test which made up the bulk of his assessment? Similarly, what teacher has not grimaced over awarding a 60% — or less — to a student who performed poorly on a major test but participated enthusiastically in the unit, worked hard on assignments — in other words, immersed herself in the business of learning?

When I look at the report cards my daughters bring home from their elementary school, I am always struck by the marked difference in the methods of reporting student progress at this level compared to those in secondary schools. For example, my daughters' report cards list a number of learning objectives students in a particular grade should achieve and, after each one, the teacher checks one of two columns: "Meeting Expectations" or "Needs Improvement." Supplementing these checklists are handwritten anecdotal comments which offer further information about the student's classroom performance. While I don't envy elementary teachers their monumental task of preparing thirty or more of these reports several times a year, I do envy them the opportunity to identify a student's specific strengths and weaknesses rather than having to quantify the student's performance with a number between zero and one hundred.

We are, however, such a number-oriented society — aren't we obsessed with interest rates, batting averages, stock exchange indexes? — that some people feel better having numbers attached to student performance. Listening to a discussion of those elementary report cards, for example, I recently overheard one parent comment, "What's with all these checkmarks? I just want to know how well my kid is doing. Is she a seventy? An eighty? A ninety?" Even the children themselves attempt to quantify their assessment, skipping over the comments and counting the number of M's (Meeting Expectations) they received and comparing their totals with those of their classmates.

Therefore, regardless how much we as secondary teachers may dislike the number-crunching quandary, it is as much a part of what we do in our classrooms as breathing. And because we *must* do it, we must *understand* what we are doing when we do it.

Assessment Versus Evaluation

The terms "assessment" and "evaluation" are sometimes used interchangeably but, since each conveys a different understanding, it is worthwhile to examine their meanings here.

Assessment is the task of gathering information about a student's performance. Teachers accumulate this information in a variety of ways, many of these involving informal observation and discussion while others include the use of more traditional assessment "tools" such as quizzes, tests, assignments, and projects. Evaluation, on the other hand, is the process by which a teacher makes sense of all this information, determining whether specific content, skill, or behavioural objectives have been achieved and whether there are weaknesses in a student's mastery of these objectives which still need to be addressed.

The issue, however, is not one of semantics. At its heart lies the answer to a question every teacher must ask: "Why do I assess in the first place?" It was, unfortunately, a question I never even thought to ask during my first few years in the classroom. I thought that assessment and evaluation were the same thing and that teachers assessed for three reasons: to bring closure to a unit of work ("We'll finish this off with a test on Friday"), to maintain control in the classroom ("You'd better pay attention because this could be on the test"), and to reward or punish students for learning or not learning ("Maybe next time you'll study harder for the test"). For me, assessment was something that ended with a mark in my record book and on a report card. Fortunately for my students, I know better now.

While there are many possible responses to the question of why teachers evaluate students, two should be foremost in a teacher's mind. First, if it is fair and appropriate, evaluation allows teachers to inform various parties about a student's progress in achieving specified learning objectives; besides the student herself, these parties include the student's parents or guardians, the student's other teachers, the school administrators, and other professionals who serve the student's interests. Second, if it is fair and appropriate, evaluation allows these parties to make informed decisions regarding the student's further education. For example, if a student's evaluation suggests she is unable to cope with certain aspects of a particular program, the teacher may wish to modify that program to enable her to achieve success with more appropriate objectives and materials. On the other hand, if a student's evaluation suggests she is capable of a more challenging program, the teacher may wish to offer enrichment alternatives that will allow her to explore more advanced materials as well as pursue personal areas of interest. Besides program modification and acceleration, other evaluation decisions may include collecting further information about a student, conferring with parents and resource personnel, procuring classroom or tutorial assistance, and many more.

It is, however, the elements of fairness and appropriateness we as educators must focus on. Not only do they preface each purpose of assessment and evaluation, they are the hallmarks of accountability.

The Question of Accountability

How often do teachers hear the cry "More accountability!" screamed by the media? Too often. Education has become the perfect political football, something everybody can toss around.

It has been blamed for the unstable economy, high unemployment, inflation, domestic violence, rising crime — in fact, just about any social ill a critic wishes to attach to it. And the person laying this blame can feel justified in doing so because everyone is an expert on education by virtue of the fact that everyone has been taught by teachers and probably knows someone who is now being taught by teachers. And everyone knows the biggest problem with education today — lack of accountability.

Each time I hear that phrase I suppress an urge to shred paper or snap pencils. Because it suggests that for decades teachers have been blithely cashing their paycheques with no concern whatsoever about their performance in their classrooms. On the contrary, I can imagine no time in history when teachers have been more concerned about their performance as well as that of their students. Given time to share concerns, teachers invariably focus on this one. During the eighteen years I have been teaching, for example, my school board has provided in-service time for teachers of similar subject areas and grade levels throughout the district to meet and discuss matters of curriculum and methodology. While the agenda of such meetings is always carefully planned, discussion has always turned to accountability — except that, until a few years ago, the term "accountability" wasn't used. More than anything, teachers wanted to know if what was happening in their classrooms was what was happening in other classrooms across the district. In essence, they wanted to know if their students "measured up" to students in other schools, in other districts — for that matter, in other countries.

Now, of course, teachers no longer have to wonder. Headlines everywhere scream that their students *don't* measure up, that teachers are doing a lousy job, and the only thing that will solve the problem is for teachers to be "more accountable." The very thing that has concerned teachers most is the very thing they are accused of having neglected.

The irony in this is that most of the people screaming for greater accountability have little or no idea how it can be accomplished. Instead, they concentrate on its measurement, on finding some means of demonstrating that teachers are or are not doing their jobs. Standardized test scores appear to be the focus of politicians and other bureaucrats intent on throwing a disgruntled public something it can sink its teeth into. When all else fails, turn to numbers. Everyone knows that the bigger the number, the better. Let's ignore the fact that few people understand what the numbers mean.

It is not my intention to debate the issue of accountability here. I believe that most teachers are doing good work in schools that are increasingly overcrowded, underfunded, and under attack from a growing number of government and corporate interests who have much to gain by convincing unhappy voters/consumers that this is not the case. Instead, it is my intent to provide teachers with a structure within which they can ensure and demonstrate their accountability, something best achieved when they focus on the purposes, means, and implications of assessment and evaluation. It is these areas that I will explore in the following chapters.

2/Knowing Where You're Going

Every summer my wife and I toy with the idea of piling our family into the car and just driving, with no destination in mind. Just four people heading down the highway discovering things about North America and ourselves, the whine of rubber on road like an anthem for our *joie de vivre*. And, of course, we never do it. By the time the car actually leaves the driveway, we've decided exactly where we want to go, how we're going to get there, and how long each leg of our journey will take.

One of the principals for whom I taught often repeated the adage "If you fail to plan, you plan to fail." While I don't as a rule cling to maxims, I agree wholeheartedly with this one. The courses we teach require countless hours of preparation, and decisions regarding overall course objectives — i.e., the learning our students should achieve — must precede all others if we are to assess our students' learning fairly and accurately.

Content Versus Intent

When a teacher is assigned a course she has not previously taught, her first thoughts often centre around the specifics of what she must teach and how she will teach them. After all, these are the "rubber meets road" moments that will comprise the more than 170 class periods she will meet the students taking her course. My first teaching assignment was in a small secondary school where I taught five different courses; the weeks prior to that first September (as well as the months following it) were filled with questions of *what* and *how*, and I spent most of my waking moments looking for the answers to these two questions. The following year involved a change in teaching assignment, and I once again turned my attention to the same

15

concerns. It took me — unfortunately — more than a few years in the classroom to realize that I teach students rather than curricula; while content is important, it is still merely the vehicle by which my students will accomplish the overall objectives that are the focus of their learning. It is these overall objectives — the *intent* of one's course — that should be the focus of every teacher's attention; concentrating on them is a far more efficient use of one's initial planning time than turning immediately to concerns of content and methodology.

I can recall, for example, spending an entire summer accumulating and organizing materials for a senior language arts course without first determining what learning I wanted my students to achieve; as it turned out, I used a fraction of the materials I had prepared, and most of those with little regard to their efficacy in relation to the course as a whole and its intended objectives. Identifying objectives — first, the overall goals of a course, and then the specific learning objectives of each unit — helps teachers focus on the *why* behind their teaching and, ultimately, guides their decisions regarding the *what* and the *how* as well as the assessment practices that will determine the extent of student achievement.

Determining Course Objectives

Unless a teacher is designing an entirely new program, course objectives will likely be prescribed by the department of education within whose jurisdiction the teacher is working. These will be stated in the department's publication of educational aims and policies and will usually be written in the form of objectives for behaviour which students should demonstrate by the end of the course. The advantage of behavioural objectives is that they offer a comprehensive statement of what students are expected to learn, which provides teachers with an overall picture of the successful learner against which their own students may be assessed.

The disadvantage of such objectives, however, is that they may devalue or even deny the possibility of other valid types of learning which may occur. For example, a specific goal of a poetry unit I taught a group of eighth-graders was to have my students recognize that poetry is image-oriented and that successful reading of it depends upon the reader's responding

16

personally to the images it evokes. One of the poems we looked at was William Carlos Williams's "Young Woman at a Window" in which a mother with tears on her cheeks sits holding a child whose nose is pressed against a windowpane. No context is offered to explain their situation, and I asked my students to create a context which the poem suggested to them. Many suggested the woman had just received word that her husband had died (some felt in an accident, others in wartime), a few decided her husband had deserted her for another woman, and still others saw her as a victim of family violence. Chris, however, responded with the statement "It's just like the video," and the next day he brought in a copy of "Sometimes She Cries," by a heavy metal band named Warrant. In the video, a young woman holds a child while her thoughts, a montage of visual images, reveal moments in a failed relationship. While my original objective was to have my students respond to poetry on a personal level, Chris had gone beyond it, recognizing — and demonstrating effectively to others — that a theme may be conveyed by more than one medium, in this case poetry, music, and film.

In seeking assistance in the identification and statement of appropriate course objectives, a teacher would benefit from the input of experienced educators around him. Ideally, a teacher should determine course objectives in consultation with the school's department supervisor or faculty head and with the principal. Department supervisors usually offer a wide range of knowledge and experience which can inform decisions regarding purpose and implementation, and the principal will have in mind basic school goals which course objectives should complement. However, with reductions in government funding of education becoming the norm, schools frequently lack department supervisors with time scheduled for such consultation, and principals often become more concerned with building management than with program development, deferring to teachers in these matters.

Lacking input from a principal or department head, teachers should feel free to approach other teachers for advice, whether in the same school or in a different district. School board superintendents should be able to identify teachers in their districts who demonstrate expertise in a particular discipline. Also, most subject areas are represented by professional associations, and a telephone call to the provincial or state headquarters of a particular association should yield the names of several teachers — active and retired — who are recognized for their contributions to their profession. Time spent with one or more of these individuals would be time well spent indeed.

A Word of Caution

As we face a new century and all the demands it places upon educators to prepare their students for it, more and more is expected of teachers. Programs continue to expand to include elements that were not part of past curricula. The calculus that I studied in university, for example, is now part of the senior secondary mathematics program; junior high science courses now include the study of personal development and relationships; language arts instructors teach media literacy. In the face of these growing demands, some teachers approach the task of determining course objectives as an exercise in condensing curriculum, identifying the minimum that can be taught successfully to ensure competent performance by students with whatever instruments are used to determine achievement. I know because I was one of those teachers. And, to some degree, I still am because — whether I agree with it or not — external testing is becoming more and more accepted as a valid means of determining school and teacher efficacy.

While teachers might argue that such testing rarely assesses what is being taught and that true learning cannot be measured by the number of shaded ovals on a machine-scored answer sheet, the reality is that a growing segment of the public perceives results from this testing as meaningful indicators of success or failure. Why shouldn't this perception be pervasive when newspapers now publish school and district scores on standardized tests, often ranking schools from best to poorest performance? If we as a profession cannot alter this perception, then we must work within its confines and structure courses that will foster growth reflected in prescribed behavioural terms. However, teachers must also allow for unexpected growth and learning in their students and must be willing not only to encourage it but, moreover, to provide a means by which it can be reflected in their evaluation of their students' learning. Subsequent chapters offer suggestions for doing both.

3 / Planning for Assessment

As a beginning teacher, I had a great sense of consequence with regard to assessment. I spent most of my time trying to catch up to where I believed I should be in a particular unit, giving little consideration to how I would assess my students' learning until I got where I was going. Often I made up tests the night before they were given, and on more than one occasion I gave an assignment during a class as an idea for one occurred to me. If I may be permitted a military metaphor, I subscribed to the scattergun method of assessment: if I kept firing long enough, I was bound to hit something.

I am not suggesting that a teacher who creates an assignment on the spur of the moment is necessarily incurring pedagogical anarchy; in fact, like the "teachable moment," the "assignable moment" often arises when a teacher suddenly discovers possibility in an untapped wellspring of student interest. I can recall, for example, a Shakespearean unit I introduced to a grade eleven class several years ago during which students asked question after question about Elizabethan life. In the middle of our discussion, I suddenly remembered an in-service conducted by George Henaut, a teacher from Pictou, Nova Scotia, who offered several suggestions for exploring the Elizabethan world and theatre, and I offhandedly mentioned to my students that it might be interesting for the class as a whole to investigate the period and present our findings to each other. Before I knew it, they and I were immersed in what became the most successful collaborative exercise to occur in my classroom. We spent that entire period and the one following it talking about what we could do and how we could do it and, for the first time, my students groaned when the bell rang. I was astonished not only by their enthusiasm but by their ingenuity as well, for resources

I had never before dreamed of were suddenly available to us: one student knew a woman whose attic was filled with theatre costumes we could borrow; another had a sister who could sew; a third had an uncle who could donate building materials; a fourth, fifth, and sixth had mothers who would donate food and even bake if necessary. My students themselves possessed skills of which I previously had been unaware — one girl was an accomplished pianist and could lay hands on sheet music appropriate for our purposes; several students were talented artists who could design and create backdrops for dramatic performances; others enjoyed singing and performing at church functions and were eager to participate in those capacities. Even the most lethargic suddenly had something to offer.

What began as a classroom activity eventually spilled over to the rest of the school and the community around it. Since so many people had so much invested in it, we opened our presentation to other classes and to the public, who came and spent an Elizabethan afternoon in the school gymnasium. They saw Queen Elizabeth I in all her royal finery begin the festivities with a speech from the throne. They were treated to reenactments of key scenes from several Shakespearean plays, among them the balcony scene from *Romeo and Juliet* performed on a parapet constructed from cardboard around the tallest ladder I had ever seen. They listened to plot summaries of plays written by the class and sung to modern tunes. They witnessed an Elizabethan court dance, musically accompanied by our pianist-in-residence and performed by eight dancers in full Elizabethan dress — including four star athletes in scarlet capes and white pantyhose. They walked through an Elizabethan landscape and attended an Elizabethan market, sampled Elizabethan food, and examined Elizabethan produce and wares. In effect, they experienced what the class had experienced — a sense of what it was like to live during the reign of the Virgin Queen and, more important, to encounter some of the world's best plays freed from the bonds of the printed page.

Of course, when it was all over I faced the task of assessing my students' work. What criteria could I measure them against? What observable indicators might enable me to translate their individual and collective efforts into percentages I could enter in my record book? Certainly none that I had predetermined. And suddenly to produce criteria for assessment *after* the work was completed would have been pointless if not perverse. So I did the only thing I felt was fair — I asked the students to assess themselves on the basis of what they had contributed to the presentation and what they had learned about Elizabethan life and theatre as a result of their efforts.

While I felt their assessment of themselves was equitable — all were very reasonable in assigning themselves a value reflective of their involvement in the unit — I began to consider how much more accurate it would have been had I informed them initially that this was the method of assessment I would use. Had they known this, they might have kept detailed accounts of the work they performed both in and out of school; also, they might have kept journals in which to reflect upon their learning — not only about Elizabethan lifestyle and theatre but about what it was like to work as a community of learners as well. Not only could my students have used these written records as tools with which to assess more accurately their roles as individuals and as members of the group, these records also would have acted as a bridge between oral performance and written language. In effect, they would have been a means by which I as a teacher could value the processes as well as the products of their learning.

As a result of that Shakespearean unit, important changes evolved in my perception of and approach to student assessment. First, I knew that I would have to plan more carefully the criteria and tools with which I would measure student performance: no longer could I give assignments and then decide how I was going to mark them. Second, I knew I would have to design an overall evaluation mechanism which would permit me to take into account far more than the few products — i.e., quizzes, projects, tests — each student might submit during a term; I needed a scheme which would also reflect commitment to learning, risk-taking, and growth as important factors in determining student success in a particular program of study. Most important, my students needed to understand from the beginning of the school year how this scheme would evaluate their success in my classroom.

Designing an Assessment Scheme

I once had a teacher who marked everything out of one hundred. Five-minute quizzes, full-period tests, month-long projects

— each and every result was recorded as a percentage which, at the end of the term or school year, was averaged equally with all the other recorded percentages. It was not unusual, therefore, for a student who scored 90% on a unit test, 90% on a major project, and 0% on a pop quiz to receive a term mark of 60%. The teacher's rationale for such a rigid approach to assessment? "This way," he explained, "my students always give me their best." Even as a high school student, I doubted that was entirely true; now, as a teacher facing a new century, I know it *couldn't* have been. To expect that students can perform to the best of their ability — on command — every task a teacher assigns is, at best, naive. At its worst, this practice results in a gross misrepresentation of student performance which flies in the face of everything we now know about the way students learn. And, while it is unlikely we would find a teacher today who assesses students in the same manner, the practice illustrates the need for a coherent and responsible scheme by which to govern student assessment.

Many school boards have in place guidelines for assessment with regard to the value which teachers may give to particular course components. For example, my own school board outlines the following options for assigning grades at the junior and senior high levels, options which teachers are required to adhere to when developing their own assessment schemes.

Junior High Assessment Guidelines		Senior High Assessment Guidelines	
Examinations	30—65%	Examinations	10—70%
Tests	15—30%	Tests	10—70%
Assignments	20—50%	Assignments	10—70%

While these guidelines offer a teacher considerable leeway — especially at the senior high level — two factors are immediately clear. First, no part of a student's overall evaluation may be based on his behaviour; gone are the days a student is given a mark for being "good" or "bad" in a classroom. After all, a teacher is responsible for evaluating student performance as measured against course objectives; how a student behaves in a classroom will not necessarily reflect the knowledge, skills, or attitudes acquired as a result of involvement in that course.

It is true that misbehaviour may be deleterious to a student's performance — for instance, a student suspended from a teacher's classroom for a period of time cannot benefit from that teacher's instruction — but that student's evaluation should reflect only performance in relation to instructional objectives. If, however, a course objective is to foster the development of particular behaviours — cooperative learning skills, for example — and the teacher has previously specified these as learning objectives, then — and only then — they may comprise part of a student's evaluation. The difference here is that a student's evaluation does not suffer as a result of negative classroom behaviour arising from conflict with the teacher or another student; it improves as a result of performing specific behaviours which the teacher has identified as valid indicators of learning.

The second factor evident in my district's assessment guidelines is a growing emphasis on a student's daily work in measuring performance. As teachers recognize and embrace a developmental perspective on learning, they recognize the need for a variety of instruments in assessing student performance fairly and accurately. Oral as well as written reports, portfolios of work as well as individual assignments, group projects as well as those submitted by a single student — all are becoming commonplace assessment tools of secondary teachers. However, the particular tools a teacher chooses to incorporate into her assessment scheme and the relative weight she will assign to each require careful consideration.

When designing an assessment scheme for a particular course and grade level, I consider four factors, the first being the nature of my learners. As a teacher at the junior high level, I consider assessment as it relates to the psychology of the adolescent; when I teach at the senior high level, I make assessment decisions in light of the emotional and cognitive profile of the young adult. Second, I consider the objectives of my course and the time I devote to each. The weight I assign particular course objectives is directly proportional to the time allotted to their achievement; a two-week unit and a six-week unit obviously do not carry the same weight in a student's overall evaluation. Third, I must bear in mind the type of learning I wish to foster in my students; will I, for example, focus on content mastery or skill acquisition or attitudinal growth or some combination of these? Having considered these three factors, I must then anticipate what this learning will look like so I can select or develop instruments which will enable me to measure my students' performance in relation to these learning objectives.

To illustrate how the first three factors shape decisions regarding assessment, I have included below the schemes I developed for two grade eight courses, language arts and math. (A detailed discussion of the selection and designing of appropriate assessment tools will be offered in subsequent chapters.) While the values assigned to various indicators of student performance differ in each, both schemes fall within the assessment guidelines as outlined by my school board.

Grade 8 Language Arts Assessment Scheme		Grade 8 Math Assessment Scheme	
Homework/Classwork	25%	Homework/Classwork	20%
Assignments	30%	Projects	10%
Tests/Quizzes	15%	Tests	20%
Exams	30%	Quizzes	10%
		Exams	40%

Because my approach to language arts instruction is developmental in focus, I allot the bulk of my students' course assessment — 55% — to work that is student-directed and process-oriented. I provide considerable class time for my students to write, to read, and to talk about writing and reading, and as a result I test infrequently. On the other hand, because I view the learning of math as more skill-oriented, I allot the bulk of my students' course assessment — 70% — to testing situations. However, I should point out that, even here, student performance is supplemented by frequent opportunity for collaborative problem-solving and test-taking.

4/Under the "B"...

During my last year of undergraduate study, I attended a party at the apartment of a classmate who was in the same secondary education program as I. While everyone else at the party was ogling his European stereo system, which cost more than the car I was driving, I was more impressed by what I found in his kitchen: a cabinet containing twenty-six small drawers, each one identified by a letter of the alphabet and containing items whose names began with that letter. For example, in the drawer marked "B" were bandages, balloons, bookends, bags of assorted sizes, and a bicycle wrench which did double-duty as a bottle opener. When I asked my host where he got the cabinet, he said he'd built it himself so he'd have "a place for everything and everything in its place." I knew then that he was going to make a good teacher.

I also knew something else: if I was going to be a good teacher, I'd have to build myself a classroom equivalent of that twenty-six-drawer cabinet to keep me organized. Rather than a collection of compartments, though, it would be a series of procedures, ways of doing things that would ensure consistency and accuracy. One would be a method of coping with disruptive classroom behaviour. Another would be a system for filing and retrieving materials useful in teaching particular concepts. Still another would be a means of planning what I would teach and how I would teach it. Yet another would be a system that would enable me to keep track of and interpret all the information I collected about student performance. If teachers are to be truly accountable to their students, to parents, to administrators, and to themselves, they must design means of doing all these things and more. The most important of these are the procedures we use to record information about what we teach and about student achievement of tasks relating to what we teach.

The Lesson Plan

I'll never understand the people who design teachers' plan books. Somehow, in a space the size of a margin, teachers are supposed to record the objectives of a lesson, the method used to achieve these objectives, a description of related activities, and possible follow-up assignments. However, if teachers are to be accountable for their teaching as well as their assessment practices, they must be able to demonstrate evidence of careful planning and preparation. The best way to do this is by writing unit plans and lesson plans which reveal careful attention to course objectives and student performance.

While there are many fine teachers who record little more than "electricity" as a lesson plan, most have prepared unit plans that are far more detailed. Unit plans help teachers focus first on the overall purpose of a unit without getting sidetracked into the questions of "what" and "how" prematurely. By concentrating on the learning I want my students to achieve during a particular unit of study, I can begin to formulate the means by which I will teach the unit as well as the means by which I will evaluate my students' learning at its conclusion. However, I believe a detailed lesson plan is crucial to demonstrating one's professional accountability.

Because I find the space in commercial plan books too limited, I create my own forms with which I plan my lessons. I design each form specifically for use in planning lessons for a particular course. The following, for example, is the form I used this year as I planned math lessons for five eighth-grade classes:

GRADE 8 MATH PLAN   LESSON #_____   UNIT _____   MONTH: _____

DATE: 8A _____   8B _____   8C _____   8S _____   8W _____

STUDENT OBJECTIVE(S):

_____

_____

_____

PROCEDURE:

Introducing the topic: _____

_____

_____

_____

_____

Teaching the lesson objective(s): _____

_____

_____

_____

_____

_____

_____

_____

_____

_____

ASSIGNMENT: _____

_____

_____

Modifications: _____

_____

_____

Once I have created a particular form I feel suits my needs, I make several photocopies of it, hole-punch them, and add them to a three-ring binder which becomes my plan book for a particular course. Any materials such as handouts, activity sheets, overhead transparencies, and so on which I use to teach a particular lesson are also hole-punched and added to the binder immediately following that lesson plan. The most obvious advantage of using this form is that it enables me to record in detail what I plan to teach and how I plan to teach it. In effect, my lesson plan becomes a script which I follow as closely as possible.

Not all teachers are fortunate enough to be able to create one lesson plan for five classes. In fact, in my eighteen years in the classroom this is the very first year I have taught only one subject and grade level. In other years I have taught as many as five different grade levels ranging from grades seven to twelve and, while scripting lessons for every class is time-consuming, it offers several advantages.

First, it helps me make efficient use of class time because in writing out the procedure I will use to teach a particular lesson, I must plan the amount of time I will spend on each of its components. Another benefit of such a script is that it enables me to teach more than one class at the same grade level the same lesson in much the same way. This is essential because, since I assess in the same manner all my classes taking the same course, they must have the benefit of the same instruction.

Another advantage of this form is that I am able to use the back of it to record notes about things which did not work well along with suggestions for improvement of the lesson. I never use exactly the same lesson plan two years in a row because these suggestions usually require me to make changes in the presentation of a concept. Also, each year my students are different and I need to draw on materials of particular interest and relevance to them. As ideas occur to me, I jot them down, often during the lesson itself.

Yet another important advantage is that this procedure provides me with a record not only of what I have taught but how I have taught it, and I can share this with interested parties — students, parents, administrators, other teachers — at any time. Students who miss school, for example, are able to find out exactly what they missed. Parents or administrators concerned about student mastery of course objectives are able to see how each lesson focuses on the teaching of particular objectives. Other teachers interested in methodology are able to see exactly how I teach a concept. While few people avail themselves of these opportunities, I believe it is my job as an educator to make these opportunities possible.

Most important, however, is the advantage this procedure

affords me in reflecting on student outcomes. If, for example, students do not perform as well on an assessed task as I would have expected, I can review my lesson plans to determine possible weaknesses in my approach to specific concepts. In this way, I am accountable not only to others but to myself as well.

Record-keeping

As teachers, we can't record everything about our students. Nor would we want to. Therefore, teachers must first decide what information is important enough to record for future reference. Obviously, any information that will influence a teacher's assessment of a student falls into this category. The most effective means I have found of recording and organizing information about student performance is an approach similar to my use of the lesson plan binder.

Like the space in commercial plan books for writing lesson plans, the space they offer for recording performance information is often too limited, consisting of rows of blocks in which teachers record scores on tests and other tasks. Limited space, however, is not their greatest weakness; they make it difficult to group and organize the information a teacher collects about students. For example, scores on unit tests and examinations are often recorded next to scores on quizzes and assignments, so it is difficult for a teacher to make a distinction between the various types of work the students are doing. As well, commercial plan books foster the assumption that student performance must always be reduced to a number which can be recorded in a block in a column. However, as I will describe in Chapter 6, students need an opportunity to experiment with exploratory tasks without the threat of being scored on all of them, yet a teacher still needs to be able to record information about their performance on these tasks.

Therefore, each year I create my own record book consisting of a three-ring binder filled with several copies of class lists of each group of students I meet. Although the school secretary compiles computer lists for every class, I prefer to make up my own because computer lists tend to be compact and I need more space than they offer. Overleaf is a portion of such a class list.

What do these class lists offer that the pages in a commercial record book do not? First, because of the spaces between the names, I can easily insert names of students who join a class later in the year. Often, commercial plan books offer no room to insert students as the year progresses. This is important because information in most schools is compiled in alphabetical order, and if I add a student's name to the end of a class list, my record of that student's work will appear out of sequence. Therefore, each time I enter scores in the computer or submit information to the office at report time, I must be careful not to enter information out of sequence.

8A											
DATE											
Aldred, Kevin											
Bower, Cindy Cochrane, John											
Dennison, Roy											
Everett, Lisa											

Also, these class lists allow me to group certain types of information regarding student performance. On one list, for example, I record scores on quizzes; on another I record information about my students' participation during in-class activities; on another I record whether students are doing homework assignments and the effort they have demonstrated in doing them (Chapter 6 provides detailed discussion and examples of this); on still another I record marks on individual, ongoing assignments such as those described in Chapter 8; on still others I record scores on tests; and so on. Following are examples of a few of these:

8A Homework/Classwork	Geological terms	Map reading activity	Questions 2, 4, 5 (p. 67)	Map exercise: climate regions	Climate graph interpretation	Paragraph: Supporting an opinion	Research notes on mountain-building	Sample book log - Joseph Howe	Questions 2, 7 (p. 45)	Reasons for/against Confederation
DATE	9/9	9/12	9/14	9/15	9/19	9/21	9/26	9/29	10/4	10/7
Aldred, Kevin	S•	S	S+	X	S	U	S	S	U	S
Bower, Cindy	S	S	S	S	S	S+	S	S	X	S
Cochrane, John	–	–	AA	S	S	U	S	S	U	S
Dennison, Roy	S	S	S	S	S	S	S	S	S	S
Everett, Lisa	S	U	X	X	S+	S	S	S	U	S+

8A Attendance										
DATE	9/6	9/7	9/8	9/9	9/12	9/13	9/14	9/15	9/16	9/19
Aldred, Kevin			A							
Bower, Cindy Cochrane, John	–	–	–	–	–					A
Dennison, Roy					A					
Everett, Lisa		A								A

This grouping of the information I record about students allows me to identify at a glance their strengths and weaknesses in relation to various components of their course work. For example, by simply turning to the list I use to record homework information, I can see whether a student is failing to attempt or to pass in work; by looking at the list on which I record test scores, I can determine if a student is coping with this form of assessment or requires more assistance in preparing for the tests that will follow. And, as I fill up a sheet, I merely add another class list and continue.

While I record information about student performance in a variety of ways, I also make it my job to record attendance every time I meet with a group of students:

8A Projects	Map: political boundaries of N.A.	Presentation: mountain-building	Relief map of North America	Book log – Joseph Howe	Debate: Confederation	Map: Confederation 1867-1949	Discussion paper: BNA Act	Role-playing: town meeting	Mock election	3 graphs: Survey of origins
DATE	9/21	10/7	10/13	10/20	10/28	11/3	11/10	11/22	12/12	1/9
Score marked out of	5	10	25	30	10	6	4	8	20	9
Aldred, Kevin	5	8	19	28	10	5	3	7	17	7.5
Bower, Cindy	4	7	22	23	9	4	3	6	18	4.5
Cochrane, John	5	9	17	26	8	6	4	8	16	8
Dennison, Roy	3	10	24	22	9	6	4	5	14	6.5
Everett, Lisa	5	10	23	27	9	5	3	4	19	9

8A Tests	Unit 1 Test	Map Test: North America	Unit 2 Test	Unit 3 Test	Unit 4 Test	Christmas Exam	Unit 5 Test	Unit 6 Test	Unit 7 Test	Unit 8 Test
DATE	9/27	10/11	10/25	11/14	12/5	12/18	1/25	2/21	3/31	4/20
Score marked out of	42	15	36	48	45	112	30	36	41	44
Aldred, Kevin	36	12	30	41	43	91	22	31	38	36
Bower, Cindy	39	14	27	45	38	87	28	30	31	30
Cochrane, John	32	14	24	36	36	101	26	32	29	33
Dennison, Roy	27	9	32	30	29	79	20	34	37	34
Everett, Lisa	36	15	28	39	41	105	29	34	40	41

This record enables me to determine if a student is responsible for completing and submitting a task on a particular date or if I should give her an extension in view of the fact that she might not have been present during preparatory work on that task. For example, in my course outline I explain that I allow students to pass in work up to two days late, but the first day late costs them 20% of the assignment's value, and two days late costs them 50%. I do not accept assignments submitted later than this unless there are mitigating circumstances such as illness, a family emergency, and so forth. If, however, a student is absent from school on a day I collect an assignment, I cannot penalize him for not submitting it; therefore, whenever I receive a late assignment, I check my attendance record to see if that student was absent.

Another benefit of the attendance record is that it helps to shed light on student performance. If a student has missed considerable class time, she will undoubtedly perform less ably than if she were present for all the classes. Also, attendance records such as these are often useful in monitoring overall student behaviour; for example, if a student is suspected of having skipped classes during a particular day, attendance records kept for each class can verify or contradict such a suspicion. In addition, as crime becomes more commonplace in schools, accurate attendance records may be required to account for students' whereabouts at particular times.

A Place for Everything. . .

Although some might feel that I "push the envelope" somewhat with regard to organization, my efforts are rewarded daily in many ways. When parents contact me about a student, I feel confident I can make an accurate assessment of his progress. When students see the emphasis I put on having "a place for everything and everything in its place," most try hard to keep themselves organized. And knowing I can lay hands on files or information at a moment's notice does much to relieve the stress associated with being a classroom teacher. (Mind you, my wife often wishes I were as organized at home — my side of our study always looks like a tornado struck it. Twice.)

5 / Great Expectations:
The First Day of School

Like a lot of parents with young children, my wife and I used to dread mealtime. Even when our daughters had progressed beyond the need for a splat mat — finally understanding that vegetables went in their mouths and not on the floor — we still viewed mealtime as an experience not unlike root canal surgery: necessary, but hardly desirable. Most of our dread stemmed from the knowledge that at some point during every meal we would be forced to take part in fairly complex negotiations: "Just three more spoonfuls of squash." "Eat two more brussel sprouts." "One more mouthful of peas and you're out of here." At times my wife and I felt more like UN arbitrators than parents, our primary function to coax our daughters to swallow at least as much food as they left on their plates.

I will always be grateful to the friend who loaned us a tape on effective parenting. Driving home one evening from a course I was taking, I slipped the tape into the car stereo and discovered the answer to the problem which our mealtime had become: expectations. Our children had come to expect they would leave some of their food on their plates; my wife and I had come to expect we would need to coax/cajole/bribe/wheedle/threaten them into eating the rest of it. Imagine the looks of surprise on our daughters' faces the following evening when we said simply, "Eat what's on your plate. If you don't, there's nothing else until breakfast." It took two meals for our children to understand that our expectations were far different than those of previous mealtimes and for me to appreciate how much I learn about teaching from being a parent.

People of all ages perform best when they know exactly what is expected of them. No adult, for example, would wish to work for an employer whose expectations regarding job performance change daily. Similarly, no student can perform to the best of her ability if she is never entirely sure what it is her teacher expects. A teacher's professional accountability begins with the understanding that all parties involved in the process of a student's education must be aware of these expectations. Not only must the teacher have a clearly conceived plan regarding the objectives of his course and how his methods of instruction and assessment will contribute to their accomplishment, but the student, her parents or guardians, the school's administrators, and the school board must also be aware of this plan. Therefore, I consider the accurate communication of these expectations to students, parents, and administrators the first task I must undertake in a school year if I am to be accountable to each of these stakeholders. This task begins the first day of school.

During the first forty-five-minute period I spend with each of the five classes I will teach in a given school year, I explain that I want them to understand three things before they leave my classroom:

1) what I expect of them,
2) what they can expect of me, and
3) what they can expect of the course I will be teaching them.

What I Expect of My Students

During the first few minutes of the class, I seat students alphabetically according to their last names. While initially off-putting for many of them, it is a strategy that offers several advantages for me as their teacher: it enables me to take attendance in seconds, it helps me to learn their names faster than if they sat in a random order, it helps redistribute some potentially undesirable combinations of students, and, most important, it facilitates my recording of homework assignments. Because my students eventually move about the room working in pairs and small groups much of the time, the alphabetical seating plan does not present a problem for them — they are often only seated in this order during the first few minutes of a lesson.

There are two ways to approach the issue of classroom rules and I've tried both. Authorities on the subject of classroom management suggest students should, in cooperation with the teacher, design their own classroom rules, something I have tried and found helpful. However, I also recognize that teachers have personal preferences about student behaviour based on their own teaching styles, and an exercise in designing their own rules can become, for some students, an exercise in guessing what the teacher will and will not allow. Therefore, in the interest of saving time and to avoid manipulating students into guessing how I feel they should behave, I prefer to identify five rules which I dictate and they write in their binders. The purpose of the dictation is to give them a written record of what I expect of them which they (and I) can refer to if the need arises.

What rules do I find necessary?

1) Bring to class the books and materials you will need.
2) Settle down to work as quickly as possible.
3) Raise your hand if you wish to speak.
4) Respect the needs and feelings of others.
5) Plan to learn, and plan to help others learn.

What My Students Can Expect of Me

When they have finished recording these rules in their binders, I tell them what they can expect of me:

1) to be fair,
2) to understand that each student is an individual whose needs may be different than anyone else's in the class,
3) never to make fun of anyone in my classroom,
4) to help each student do as well as he or she can, and
5) to reward students for working hard and working well.

I then explain that, if anyone ever has reason to feel I am not doing each of these things, she is to let me know as soon as possible, usually at the end of class or during free time. Teachers are human and we make mistakes, and I want my students to understand that I appreciate people who make me aware of mine. By that same token, I explain that I will remind them if they are not following each of the rules I've given them, and I explain the process I follow.

If, for example, a student behaves in a way that I find disruptive, I write his or her name on the board. I make no comment and continue with the lesson — the name on the board is simply a signal to this student that he or she has been warned. If the student stops being disruptive, no further action is taken. If, however, the student continues to be disruptive, I put a check-mark beside his or her name. If the disruptive behaviour still continues, more checkmarks are added. The following is an explanation of the consequences each checkmark carries with it:

✔ The student is given a note to take home explaining that he/she has been disruptive. (See Appendix A.) A parent or guardian must sign the note and the student must bring it to class the next day. The student may not be allowed to return to class until the signed note is returned.

✔ ✔ On the *following* school day at 12:35 the student must come to my classroom and spend fifteen minutes in detention. The student may not be allowed to return to my class until the detention has been served.

✔ ✔ ✔ On the *following* school day at 12:35, the student must come to my classroom and spend thirty minutes in detention. The student may not be allowed to return to my class until the detention has been served.

✔ ✔ ✔ ✔ The student is sent to the Vice-Principal's office where further action is taken.

NOTE: These checkmarks are not carried over from one day to the next — every student begins with a clean slate each day.

In the several years I have used it, no student has ever received four checkmarks in a single class period, and only a handful have ever received three.

I find it extremely important that parents understand the system that I use, and I send home a letter (a copy of which appears in Appendix B) on the first day for them to read so I can involve them directly in the process. Most parents appreciate knowing what is expected of their children, and they support a teacher's efforts to create a learning environment that is free from disruptions.

What My Students Can Expect of the Course

Once I have established what I expect of my students and what they can expect of me, I distribute an outline of the course. I view a course outline as a businessperson might view a contract: as a statement of intent and an explanation of the conditions that govern the parties involved. While course outlines vary from teacher to teacher in length and appearance, the best include five types of information:

1) the objectives of the course,
2) the texts and/or other source materials that will be used to achieve those objectives,
3) required materials students will need to purchase for use in the classroom and at home,
4) the teacher's assessment scheme, and
5) suggestions that will ensure a student's success in that course.

Some teachers also include a breakdown of course content, often listing the various units the course will encompass and the time frame allotted to each. One advantage of the inclusion of such a breakdown is that it enables both teacher and student to view course content as it relates to course objectives — while the goals of each unit will be specific to that segment of the curriculum, they must reinforce the overall objectives which are the course's *raison d'etre*. Another advantage is that this breakdown affords students a sense of where they are going and how long it will take to get there.

Years ago I took a short course on time management — something else which parenthood necessitated — and it remains one of the most helpful I have ever taken. Not only did the instructor offer numerous organizational tips ("Make and priorize a 'To Do' list at the end of every day") and suggestions for improving efficiency ("Never handle a piece of mail more than once"), he eloquently demonstrated all of them by completing the entire two-day course in a day and a half. Two suggestions he offered to administrators involved staff meetings:

1) Never conduct a meeting without a purpose.
2) Always distribute an agenda to people in attendance.

Teachers spend — seemingly — half their lives in meetings, and people who have attended any that lacked both an obvious purpose and an agenda will recall the pointless eternities they became. If this is true of a two-hour meeting, we surely can understand the need for a clear statement of both at the beginning of a course which spans an entire school year or semester, especially when some participants in that course may be less than enthusiastic about their involvement in it.

Some Suggestions for Writing the Course Outline

While a clearly articulated course outline is an essential tool for guiding assessment and ensuring success and accountability on the part of both teacher and student, it is also an opportunity for the teacher to demonstrate her professionalism and to model the qualities she wants to encourage in her students' work and behaviour. With this in mind, I offer the following suggestions for writing this document:

1) Prepare the outline in a professional, attractive manner. Avoid handwriting course outlines — use a computer with a laser printer; if this isn't available, use a typewriter with a good-quality ribbon.
2) Write the outline in complete sentences and paragraphs. A document that will guide student learning should reflect the importance of the written word in form as well as in content.
3) Explain as clearly as possible what it is you want to say. Use concrete nouns and active verbs, and avoid wordiness — the adage "less is more" is appropriate here. Share a first draft of your outline with a friend or colleague whose opinion you value and ask for a response to both its content and the language you have used.
4) Organize information under headings so that key ideas stand out and are easy to find.
5) Edit your outline carefully for all writing errors, especially mistakes in usage and spelling. Educators whose writing is filled with errors lack credibility with students, their parents, and administrators.

Some Final Words about First Days

Some teachers might be appalled by the fact that at the end of the first day I have not passed out a textbook or assigned work or done any of the other things that are usually associated with the first day of school. I don't see this as a problem. I believe I have concentrated on more important tasks which, if I have performed them well, will set the tone for all the other days I will meet these classes.

6/Assessing Process

"Haven't you finished yet?" I ask as I clear dishes from the dining-room table.

Eight-year-old Caitlin studies her broccoli, probing with her fork what is now a cold, green mass. She looks up at me. "Not yet," she sighs.

I sigh, too. "Caitlin, can you tell me why you're always the last person to finish her meal?"

She doesn't pause a moment. Smiling, she chirps, "*Somebody* has to be last, Daddy."

And, of course, she's right. Somebody *does* have to be last.

Like most parents, I don't involve myself in formal assessment of my children; I prefer the informal and much more histrionic "suffering martyr" assessment: "If I had a penny for every time I've told you to clean up this room..." followed by a roll of eyes heavenward and a slow, sad shake of the head. If, however, I *were* to engage in formal assessment, the criterion I would most likely use as an indicator of successful performance would be a commitment to task demonstrated by the completion of a given activity within X minutes. If I were to assess Caitlin solely in terms of her performance at dinnertime, she would no doubt score the lowest in our family.

But Caitlin is first out of bed in the morning, even on weekends, while her sister and parents burrow further under their blankets. She's the first outside to play, the first to build a snowman in the winter and a teepee in the summer, the first to go to sleep at night in any season. If I were to use the same criterion to assess her performance in these other activities, she would score higher than any other family member. *No one* is last in *everything*.

This, of course, is the reason why teachers need to employ

a variety of assessment methods in determining student achievement of course objectives. Some students do not — for a variety of reasons — perform well on full-period tests yet have little difficulty with take-home projects requiring mastery of the same material. Others, given a few days to complete a project, may struggle with disorganization and the tyranny of a deadline yet focus well on the immediate requirements of an in-class test. Few people respond equally well to all tasks, and if a teacher is to assess students fairly and accurately, he must provide them with a variety of opportunities to demonstrate what they know and what they can do. While I cannot begin to describe all the tasks teachers use in their assessment of student performance, I group them into two categories: assigned work and testing situations. This chapter will address several issues relating to the first of these.

Problems with Assignments

Any athlete knows that the way to master a skill is to practice it, preferably in the company of someone who can reinforce what she is doing correctly and make suggestions for how to improve her performance. Teachers design and sequence countless classroom activities and homework assignments with the same understanding in mind: to help students learn the skills and content they encounter in class.

There are, however, three problems inherent in the use of classroom activities and homework assignments, all involving students' perception of them. First, many students view such tasks as endless busywork rather than opportunities for learning and, as a result, some may choose not to do them and others may perform with such indifference that the desired learning is not achieved. Second, some students perceive homework and classwork as searches for the Holy Grail: exercises in identifying the elusive single "answer" — which the teacher knows and they must guess — rather than occasions for possibility, for open-ended exploration of a topic or issue. Finally, by the time they reach secondary school, many students have been conditioned to believe that if an activity or assignment does not receive a mark or does not in some concrete way contribute to a mark, it is unimportant. Unfortunately, because most secondary teachers see well over a hundred students each day, they cannot possibly respond to and accurately assess all the work produced by those students. Thus, while classwork and homework are as much a part of teaching and learning as breathing, secondary teachers must at some point tackle the three-headed demon which assignments spawn.

Making Assignments Meaningful

The first problem — the perception of assignments as pointless busywork — is most easily addressed because much classwork and homework *is* busywork, tasks given to fill up class time, to demonstrate to parents and administrators that students are working, and to provide a series of scores which can be manipulated into a percentage at the end of a term. I know this because no one is more guilty of having assigned busywork than I. For years I believed that if my students were not producing something — anything — then I wasn't doing my job. Complaints such as "Why do we have to do this, anyway?" fell on deaf ears, the expression on my face conveying my unspoken "Because I said so." It wasn't until I read an article suggesting teachers try doing a few of their own assignments that I began to question their purpose and validity. Since then, I have attempted to make the work I assign more meaningful by focusing on three questions:

1) What learning do I want this assignment/activity to promote or reinforce?
2) How will this assignment/activity promote or reinforce this learning?
3) Would I want to do this assignment/activity?

While it is certain that few — if any — assignments will appeal to all students, there are things teachers can do to increase their relevance for students:

1) Build interest in the concept that gives rise to an assignment. Don't underestimate the power of storytelling and shared experience in making students receptive to a task. For example, the period I spent with a senior class talking freely about questions we'd like answered laid the foundation for what culminated in a major research project.
2) Clearly state the connection between the assignment and the intended learning objective. When students understand the

"why" behind an activity, they are more likely to recognize its value and to participate in it willingly.

3) Extend the assignment beyond the classroom. Be prepared for questions like "When are we ever going to use this?" Map-reading skills seem more significant when viewed in the context of real situations such as planning a motor trip to destinations students would like to visit. Likewise, the format of a business letter becomes important when students are writing real letters to real people for real purposes.

4) Encourage students to suggest alternative assignments. As long as they result in the intended learning, it does not matter who conceives them. Some of my most effective assignments are those which students have invented.

5) When an assignment serves merely as a vehicle for practicing a skill (combining like terms in algebraic expressions, for example), limit the number of questions required. If a student can do five, she most likely can do fifteen or fifty.

6) Offer a variety of assignments aimed at different levels of student ability so that more capable students are challenged and less capable students are not overwhelmed. Just as we are suspicious of clothing labels which read "One size fits all," teachers should be cautious about assigning the same task to all learners.

7) Allow students to demonstrate their learning in a variety of ways. Most often we require students to demonstrate their learning through writing and we overlook the possibilities inherent in speech, music, art, drama, dance, and so on. During their study of Dickens's *Great Expectations*, my grade twelve students and I were astonished and thrilled by a character sketch of Miss Havisham prepared by Julie, who, wearing a yellowed wedding dress and one shoe, raspily recounted the event that destroyed her life.

8) Make students a part of the assessment process. Involve them in determining the criteria that will be used to assess them. Create opportunities for students to assess themselves.

These ideas will be discussed further in subsequent chapters.

Debunking the Holy Grail

For students, assignments can become little more than exercises in guessing what a teacher already knows. Knowledge is seen as a commodity, something that can be processed, packaged, and delivered to consumers like canned corn or freeze-dried coffee. But knowledge, of course, is much more than that. It is the understanding that results from interaction rather than transmission, interaction with textual material, with other individuals, with the environment, and so on. Understanding occurs when a concept or idea is viewed in a context that has particular meaning for the individual.

For example, my wife and I had repeatedly told then three-year-old Lauren that light bulbs were hot and should be avoided, but she only fully understood our warning the evening she got out of bed, turned on her lamp, and tried to remove the burning bulb. When I questioned her the following day about the angry blister on her finger, she explained what had happened and how she had crawled back into bed without making a sound. When I asked her why, she replied, "I thought you would be mad." The image of her lying in pain in the darkness haunts me still, but even more disturbing was her reason for doing so — her belief that I would punish her for making a mistake. But why should this have surprised me? After all, I'd spent years punishing students for the mistakes they made while doing the tasks I had assigned them.

Just as a basketball coach does not expect a rookie to sink every shot, neither can a teacher expect her students to complete every assigned task successfully. While the coach and teacher might hope that this happens, it would be unrealistic — and, no doubt, counterproductive — to insist upon it; instead, learners need ample opportunity for practice, continued encouragement, and appropriate feedback which will enable them to determine strengths and weaknesses in their efforts. Teachers must design both assignments and assessment strategies with these points in mind.

Also, if assignments — especially those involving initial exposure to a concept or skill — are to promote learning rather than Holy Grail seeking, they should encourage students to consider alternative solutions to problems, pursue other avenues of inquiry — even dead ends — rather than proceed lockstep toward a teacher's answer. Teachers must applaud divergent thinking and give credit for it in their assessment.

Besides applauding alternative methods of approaching an assignment, teachers need to design assignments for which there are no known answers. In the study of fiction, for example, students often examine the choices writers make in telling a story. Questions such as "Why does the character do this?" tend to "close down" a story, while questions like "What else might the character have done?" open it up and allow students to see writing as a process of possibility, of choice-making, rather than a linear endeavour.

Making Everything Count

"Does this count?"

I used to rankle every time I heard this question. "Yes, it counts," I'd hiss through clenched teeth. Because I knew what was coming.

"How much?"

"Twenty points."

"Is that twenty points for the term or twenty points for this assignment averaged in with all the other assignments?"

"Twenty points for this assignment."

"How much is that on the whole term?"

"That depends."

"Depends on what?"

"On how many other assignments I give you this term."

"How many other assignments are you giving us?"

And on and on while the vein in my right temple threatened to explode.

I used to think that the initial question — "Does this count?" — was motivated entirely by laziness. After all, if a student were willing to work hard, it wouldn't matter whether a task counted or not, would it? But, of course, things are not so simple. Yes, there is an element of laziness which factors into the question — what teacher, for example, has not tossed a questionnaire into the wastebasket after seeing it required an anonymous response? — but there are other concerns which motivate this query.

Chief among them are the many other demands on the time of a secondary student. Besides the assignments given by as many as six or seven other teachers, there are commitments to athletic teams and other extra-curricular groups, responsibilities to family and friends, possibly a part-time job. And somewhere in there the student might even want the opportunity to do something besides work — leisure time, perhaps? There are so many things vying for the attention of the secondary student that no teacher can blame her for asking "Does this count?" The teacher who still might wish to levy that blame has only to think of the demands he himself faces each day to recognize that no one can do it all, that we all function according to priority and the items on the lower end of that priority list are the things we leave undone. Since a major goal of education is to prepare students for the adult world of work and play, the question "Does this count?" shouldn't upset us because it reflects the efforts of a person learning to prioritize.

Because work that does not count tends to fall toward the bottom of students' priority lists, teachers feel pressured to make *everything* count. "If I don't mark it, they won't do it!" is the complaint most often moaned over an elbow-high stack of assignments in the staffroom. Having taught language arts for sixteen years, I'm familiar with the bundle/sack/case/trunk that English teachers lug with them everywhere. However, adapting an idea I discovered in *The English Journal*, I have devised an assessment strategy which — for me — answers the question "How do I make everything count and not go crazy in the process?" This strategy allows me to cope with great volumes of student work and, at the same time, to encourage risk-taking and hard work without penalizing students for making mistakes.

The Strategy

First, I make a distinction between homework/classwork tasks and tasks I call projects, which receive a numerical mark based on predetermined criteria. The former involve exploratory assignments which introduce students to a concept as well as assignments which require them to practice a skill to encourage proficiency, and are not marked numerically. I give my students at least one of these tasks each day, often as a group task to complete during class time and/or at the end of a class to complete individually before we meet again. Projects grow out of this exploratory or practice work, and students have more time to complete these, often with the benefit of peer support as well as help from me. I will discuss projects further in Chapter 7.

At the beginning of the school year, I provide students with a detailed explanation regarding how I will assess homework/

classwork tasks. The following appeared in the course outline I gave my eighth-grade math students:

I don't think it is fair to assess everything a student does (especially when he or she is still in the process of learning). However, since I consider all the work you do to be important, I *will* check to see that homework and classwork have been completed and skills have been mastered. Often I will check the work as I walk about the room, and sometimes I will collect the work to check it more closely. I will not put a numerical value on this work; instead, I will use one of the following symbols which I will record in my book:

S   satisfactory effort (you have attempted all the assignment and have shown your work). NOTE: YOU MAY HAVE MADE ERRORS BUT I AM PLEASED WITH THE EFFORT I SEE.

S +   exceptional effort (not only have you completed the assignment, but you have taken special care in organizing your work and presenting it neatly or you have done even more than I assigned)

U   unsatisfactory (you have not done all the assignment, OR your work is so messy that it is unacceptable)

X   you did not have the assignment done when I asked to see it, OR you did not show your work (I give no value for answers unless you show *how* you arrived at them)

Your homework/classwork mark will be determined by my record of the homework and classwork you do during the term. If you complete all homework and classwork assignments in a satisfactory (S) manner, you will receive 16 of the possible 20 points. If all work is completed and some of it is exceptionally well done (S +), this mark will be higher. If work is unsatisfactory or incomplete (U or X), this mark will be lower.

Part of your homework will be to bring all the necessary materials to class. Another part of your homework will be to keep your math binder neat, organized, and up-to-date, and occasionally I will check your binder to see if you are doing this. Please see the sheet titled "ORGANIZING YOUR MATH BINDER" for details about your binder. [See Appendix C]

A FEW WORDS ABOUT LATE HOMEWORK: Because your homework/classwork mark is given primarily for your EFFORT, part of this effort will be to make sure you have your work ready when I call for it. I do not accept late homework, even if it's only in your locker. Therefore, before coming to school each day, make sure you have that day's assignment in your binder in the appropriate place (following the lesson on that material).

Why award a 16 out of 20 rather than a 20 out of 20 to a person who has done all that I have asked? Actually, for these exploratory tasks, I insist only that students demonstrate effort toward achieving a particular goal. I do not expect polished work — students may work rapidly and, consequently, may make several errors. I believe 16 out of 20 points (80% of the homework mark) is sufficient reward for simply accomplishing the tasks; at the same time, it allows me room to reward others who do more than is required. Most teachers can recognize easily work that has been dashed off at the last moment with little thought, and I record a U (unsatisfactory) for these.

The advantage of being able to assess a homework or classwork assignment solely in terms of effort is that I can do so very quickly. If I intend to have students share responses to an assignment in class, I will walk about the room prior to this and record in my record book whether the work has been done — even with a class of thirty or more students, I can accomplish this in three or four minutes. If I wish to see how well each individual has handled a particular task, I will ask students to pass in their assignments so I can look at them more closely. Since I am not assigning them numerical marks — a process that takes considerable time as it involves assessing each assignment in terms of specific criteria — I can skim them quickly to determine whether the majority of students have understood the concept or whether I need to re-teach it to all or a few.

Another advantage of this assessment strategy is that it also enables me to assess students according to how well they work in class. Much of the instruction I provide is in small-group settings, and I require my students to perform certain roles to ensure that their groups stay on task. Whether they accomplish the task successfully or not is of less importance to me than their ability to remain on task and be supportive of each other. If an individual performs her group role effectively, I record S by her name for that task; if an entire group works cooperatively, I record S + by each group member's name.

A third advantage is that this system allows me to reward students for demonstrating a commitment to learning. In math, for example, I give a bonus mark (+) to students who take extra care in organizing the work leading to a solution. In language arts, I give bonus marks to students who demonstrate extra effort in an assignment; for example, to introduce the clipped nature of dialogue, I assigned my students to record and transcribe a one-minute portion of a conversation, and Jennifer transcribed more than twice that amount and earned a bonus for doing so. In all my courses, I give bonus marks to students who demonstrate initiative and insight, whether it be in an assignment or during work in class. Finally, I reward with bonus marks students who make connections between what we are doing in school and life outside the classroom, connections that take the form of newspaper articles, cartoons, anecdotes, and so on. For example, during a social studies unit on nineteenth-century immigration in Canada, Meredith brought in a book she'd found containing political cartoons that vividly depicted the plight of Eastern European immigrants tricked by a government colonization scheme into coming to Canada and settling the West. Not only did Meredith make an important connection between our work in class and other media, the book she brought to class enabled us to examine the role of political satire as a force for heightening awareness and promoting change.

A fourth advantage of this system is that it provides me with a means of assessing the processes as well as the products of students' learning.

The most important advantage, however, is that people who have difficulty demonstrating proficiency on tests and more formal assignments are able to accumulate considerable value which can offset low marks in those areas; conversely, a bright student who does well on tests and formal assignments but is not committed to the business of learning — i.e., does not choose to work daily — will find his end-of-term mark much lower than his ability level would warrant. I delight in telling my classes that every homework/classwork task can be done incorrectly and a student can still receive an excellent assessment for that portion of the term mark because right answers are secondary to an individual's commitment to learning.

Arriving at a Mark

At the beginning of the school year, I check homework assignments every day to demonstrate the importance I place on having them done. As the year progresses, I may check homework less frequently — depending on the scope of a lesson and the time it will require, I may not have time to check every day — but it becomes even more important then for students to have their work done. For example, if I check homework ten times and a student has failed to complete two of these assignments, she will have lost 20% of her homework mark for that period. If I check homework only six times and she has failed to complete two assignments, she will have lost 33% of her homework mark for that period; hence, the fewer times I check homework, the more each assignment is worth, so students recognize the effect of failing to do homework assignments at any time. During the first week of school, I demonstrate the impact of their daily work on their term mark by showing an overhead of a homework record from a previous year and discussing how I calculated a mark based on this record.

At the end of a reporting period, I will have recorded numerous symbols by each person's name and from these symbols I will arrive at a numerical value which amounts to 20% of that reporting period. The following is an example of such a record over a three-week period:

8A Homework/ Classwork	Activity: How Big Is a Million?	Pp. 10-11: #4, 6, 10	Activity: How to Solve a Problem	Pp. 15-16: #8, 11, 12	Pp. 18-19: #2-69	Groupwork: Trouble-Shooting Problems	Pp. 22-23: #5, 6, 8	Activity: Wading through Information	Groupwork: Working with Money	Pp. 31-32: #8-12	P. 55: #2-5	Activity: Front-end Strategy	Activity: Estimating
DATE	9/8	9/9	9/12	9/13	9/14	9/16	9/19	9/20	9/21	9/23	9/26	9/28	9/29
Erin O.	S	S	S	S	S	S	S	S	S	S	S	S	S
John P.	S	S	U	S	X	X	U	S	X	S	S	S	X
Amy R.	S	S+	S	S+	U	S+	S	X	S+	U	S+	X	S+
Colin T.	S	S	A	AA	S	X	U	S+	S	U	S+	S	X
Susan W.	S	S+	S+	S	S+	S+	S	S+	S	S+	S+	S	S+

Since 16 is the score a student receives out of 20 if she completes all the tasks satisfactorily, I awarded Erin a 16 for this time period. Not all students complete all the tasks, but unless a consistent pattern emerges, I do not give students a hard time about not having completed a homework assignment; I understand that, on a particular evening, my course may have had a lower priority than other commitments (school-oriented and otherwise). However, my students must also be prepared to accept the consequence which is an X in my record book. If a student repeatedly fails to have homework done, I speak to him about it and, if there is no immediate improvement, I call home. Parents appreciate these calls, especially when I can give them specific dates when homework was not done. Most parents hear the line "I don't have any homework" more times than they care to believe, but without a call such as this, they have no reason to intervene in their son's or daughter's study habits. By the time a report card arrives home with a term mark that reflects a problem with homework, a student may have lost too much ground to regain. Most parents prove to be willing allies in encouraging such students to take part in the business of learning.

Sometimes a student is absent when I check homework, so I will record an A by her name. However, when she returns to school, she must show me — or pass in — the assigned work or that A becomes an X. Similarly, a student may not have homework completed because he was absent on the day it was assigned, so I will record an AA by his name. He will have one day more than the period he was absent to make up this work or that AA becomes an X. In the example above, Colin failed to show me two such assignments and, at the end of the reporting period, received an X for each.

In determining a numerical value for students who do less — or more — than the satisfactory requirement, I first count the number of times I checked homework or recorded the results of an in-class task, then divide this number into 16 — the value of an S for each task — to determine how many points each task is worth. If I check homework/classwork 19 times during a reporting period, I divide 16 by 19 to get 0.84, which will become the value of each S during this period. In the above example, I checked 13 tasks; since 16 divided by 13 is 1.23, this will be the value of each S. I consider a U and a + to be worth half an S, so in adding up the symbols for each of the four remaining students, treating each S as equal to 1, and each U and + as .5, I arrived at the following preliminary totals:

John   8 (7 S's = 7, 2 U's = 1)
Amy   13 (9 S's = 9, 2 U's = 1, 6 +'s = 3)

```
Colin    9 (7 S's = 7, 2 U's = 1, 2 +'s = 1)
Susan   17 (13 S's = 13, 8 +'s = 4)
```

Multiplying each total by 1.23, I get the following marks, each out of 20:

John	9.8
Amy	16
Colin	11.1
Susan	20.9

Note that Susan scored more than 20 out of 20, a mark which I allowed to stand. Also, note that Colin missed as many assignments as John but scored higher than John because of the bonus marks he earned. When students recognize the effect that bonus value has on a term mark, most place a high priority on my homework assignments. As a result, students in my courses perform better for me than did those students whom I taught prior to developing this system.

A final comment about this system involves the issue of accountability. Often at the end of the first reporting term a student — and sometimes his parents — will ask me to justify my assessment of the homework/classwork component of her term mark. I first refer them to the explanation I give at the beginning of the year which outlines how these marks are calculated, then I show them my record of that student's performance on these tasks, and, finally, I do the math that leads to that score. While they may not like the mark, all understand that this is no arbitrary score I've pulled out of my head. It reflects — as accurately as I can manage — my assessment of their commitment to learning in my classroom.

Accountability Versus Accounting

While this method may appear highly technical at first glance, it actually is simple to use. Not only does it provide a mechanism by which I can give my students value for attempting a task without penalizing them for making mistakes, it effectively conveys the understanding that everything "counts." Any teacher considering using it should, however, demonstrate to his students how scores will be calculated so they will understand how failing to do homework or classwork will impact directly on term marks.

7 / Assessing Product

Often when teachers face the task of assessing a product —
whether it be a project or presentation or performance or test
question — they find things they didn't expect to be there.
Sometimes they are pleasant surprises, sometimes they are not:
a student has misunderstood the task and produced a result far
different than the teacher requested; another has misunderstood
the concept and performed far less capably than expected; yet
another has included information or materials which, while
demonstrating considerable effort, are not specifically related
to the task; and so on. It is these surprises that make the assigning of marks to students' work the most difficult part of
assessment.

I enjoy teaching. I enjoy the fact that no two days are ever
the same. I enjoy planning my lessons, trying to find new and
interesting ways to present the same ideas. I enjoy the students
who come into my room and challenge me, make me justify
what it is I do and why. I even enjoy the drudgery of photo-
copying and collating and hole-punching (after a seven-period
day with extra help at noon, there's something wonderfully
mindless about collating and hole-punching). But I hate marking. Because it's personal. And pernicious. Beside every percentage or letter grade we assign there's an invisible stamp that
all students see clearly: "THIS IS WHAT YOU ARE WORTH." And as
much as we might say, "I am assessing your *work*, not *you*,"
our students think differently. *They* are the walking 90's, 80's,
65's, 40's. Try as we might to change that perception, it is there.
Teachers know. They feel it every time they return to students
something with a mark on it, see it demonstrated vividly as
students flip pages, ignore written comments, race to find the
value written in red at the end, fold down the corner so no one

else can see, reveal it slowly, then beam or scowl or crumple the paper in white fists.

As much as anything else, it was this feeling that led me to design the homework/classwork assessment scheme I described in Chapter 6 which requires that I determine only if an assignment demonstrates satisfactory effort. Yes, students still turn rapidly to see if I've written an S or a U (or an S +), but few are ever surprised by what they find. They *know* if they've put effort into an assignment. And they know *I* know.

Yet, at some point I, too, have to assess product, have to assign a value to a project or a test answer or some other endeavour I've designed to determine the level of achievement each student has reached at various points in the courses I teach.

Preparing to Assess Product

In designing a task — project, presentation, test, etc. — which will receive a mark representing a specific portion of the term or year, I consider the following questions:

1) Why am I assigning this task? Will it assist my students in learning or extending their understanding of particular concepts or skills? Will it assist me in determining how effectively my students have learned particular concepts or skills?
2) What specific knowledge or skills must students use in successfully completing this task?
3) Are my students capable of performing this task? Must I modify it for academically challenged students? Should I provide enrichment alternatives for gifted students?
4) What must I do to prepare my students for this task? How can I do this most effectively?
5) Will students work individually or collaborate in groups? Will they each produce a single response to the task, or is it more appropriate that each student contribute to a group response?
6) How much time must I allot for students to complete the work satisfactorily? Must I allow class time or can I expect that all this can be accomplished out of class?
7) Would I want to perform this task? If not, what can I do to make the task more relevant, more appealing?

After making these decisions, I consider the following questions regarding the assessment of this task:

1) What will a successful response to the task look like? What criteria will I use to determine if students have performed well?
2) Will all students be assessed according to the same criteria, or do performance expectations vary according to student ability?
3) Do my students understand what a successful response to the task will look like? How can I help them understand the criteria I will use to assess their performance?
4) If students collaborate on a group response, will all group members receive the same mark, will I assess each student's individual contribution to that response, or will their assessment be a combination of both?
5) Will I assess only the final response to the task, or will I also assess the process by which students arrive at this response?
6) What part will this task play in my overall assessment of students' performance? What weight will it carry in relation to other tasks I have assigned?
7) Would I want to be assessed in this manner? Would I have sufficient opportunity to demonstrate what I know and can do?

While the number of considerations appears at first overwhelming, these questions nonetheless represent the variety of issues that must be addressed when teachers decide to assess a product.

Addressing the Issues: A Language Arts Example

One of the most important decisions a writer makes when writing a story is the choice of who will tell it because point of view shades or colours the narrative and influences a reader's perception of events. Because readers should be conscious of this influence, language arts curricula include the teaching of this concept; I have, for example, taught it to students — with varying performance expectations — at both the junior and senior high levels. The following account describes how I addressed the issues outlined above in teaching and assessing my eighth-grade students' understanding of point of view.

Basic to all of my considerations were three learning objectives I wanted my students to achieve:

1) to recognize the various points of view a writer may use to tell a story,
2) to identify the advantages and limitations of each point of view, and
3) to determine how a writer's choice of viewpoint influences the reader's perception of events which occur in a story.

I knew that, whatever I chose to have my students do in their study of this concept, I would have to concentrate on helping them develop the skills that would enable them to accomplish these three objectives.

To begin, I assigned the students to investigate the following scenario in small groups and to present their findings to the class the following day:

EYEWITNESSES

Tommy Smith, a six-year-old boy, has been hit by a car and rushed to the hospital by ambulance. Below is a sketch of the scene of the accident.

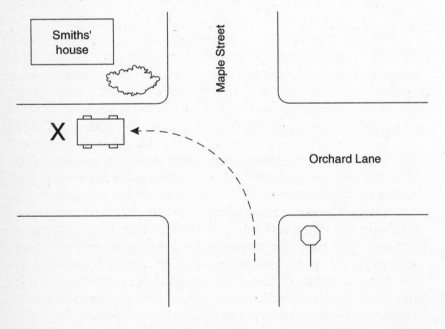

A policeman has arrived on the scene to take the statements of the people who witnessed the accident. Three people saw the accident:

1) Frank Connors, the driver of the car that hit Tommy — he's a traveling salesman and can't afford to lose his license;
2) Ellen Smith, Tommy's mother, who dislikes Frank Connors — Frank sold her an expensive vacuum cleaner that broke down shortly after she bought it;
3) Harry Willows, a tourist passing through the town.

The following are facts about the accident:

— the accident happened at 11:10 a.m.
— Tommy was playing with a ball on the lawn in front of his house
— Harry was out for a walk and was standing on the corner waiting to cross the street
— Ellen was sweeping off the sidewalk in front of her house
— Frank was in his car turning left from Maple Street onto Orchard Lane
— there is a large lilac bush on the edge of the Smiths' lawn that blocks the view of the street
— the ball bounced into the street
— Frank was late for a sales appointment
— there is a stop sign on Maple Street
— there was no other traffic on either street at that time

TASK: Write the reports given by each of the three witnesses.

Working in their small groups, the students prepared three eye-witness accounts of this single incident. While each group presented unique witness statements, similarities were evident among the groups' efforts: the "Ellen Smith" accounts placed the blame fully on Frank Connors, the "Frank Connors" accounts placed the blame completely on the careless victim, and the "Harry Willows" accounts shared the blame between driver and victim.

Following the presentations, I asked the class to consider the difficulty a police officer must face in weighing conflicting witness accounts of a crime, and I asked them to select the witness they would be most inclined to believe had they been the investigating officers. All identified Harry Willows as the most believable and, when I asked why, they responded, "Because he didn't know Frank or Ellen or Tommy. He didn't have anything to gain by lying." Having elicited this response, I introduced the concept of point of view and explained how a writer's choice of who will tell her story is important for the same reason: if a narrator is directly involved in the events of a story, he may not give as unbiased an account of them as a narrator who is completely uninvolved. For homework, I asked the students to skim over a few of the stories in their literature text to identify whom the writers had chosen to tell them.

The following class, their discussion of the reading assignment led my students to identify two main points of view: "third-person," in which a writer uses a narrator who is not actually in the story to tell it (as one student put it, "He's like Harry Willows — just an observer"); and "first-person," in which a writer uses one of the story's characters to tell it.

Over the next few classes, we looked at several short stories featuring different kinds of narrators. Finally, I assigned the task of rewriting a portion of a story told in the third person as a first-person narrative by the main character.

After answering questions about the task, I asked the students if they understood its purpose. What, in effect, did I want to know about what they had learned? Most students immediately recognized that I wanted to see if they understood the difference between the two points of view well enough to be able to change the story from one point of view to another. Others realized that changing the viewpoint would require getting to know the main characters better and showing this through his thoughts and feelings. I also reminded them about other criteria I had used to assess previous writing assignments: neatness and mechanics. I told them they would have class time and peer support for revising and editing their projects, and I gave them the following assessment sheet which they were to attach to their final draft:

POINT OF VIEW PROJECT	WEAK	FAIR	STRONG	OUTSTANDING
APPEARANCE				
1. The assignment is neat and presented in the proper form.	1	2	3	4
CONTENT				
2. The assignment is written entirely in first-person point of view.	2	4	6	8
3. The writer has taken the reader inside the mind of the main character to SHOW why he behaved the way he did.	3	6	9	12
EDITING				
4. The writer has edited carefully for all the writing errors studied so far.	2	3	5	6

TOTAL: _____
30

Assessing the Assessment Mechanism

While few of us would consider ourselves connoisseurs of fine food, most of us feel capable of judging whether a meal has been prepared with skill or merely thrown together to satisfy the most basic requirements for human sustenance. It is when we are called upon to assess the relative success of one dish over another, however, that we are less certain of our abilities. In the same way, teachers easily recognize when a student's response to an assignment or test question demonstrates basic understanding of the concept involved, but they may find it much more difficult — and time-consuming — to assign a value reflecting the relative merits of one response over another. This is one reason why I create rubrics to help me arrive at the mark I will give a student for a particular assignment.

There are, however, other advantages of using the rubric:

1) It enables me to focus on the original learning objectives the assignment was designed to assess.
2) It enables students to focus on these same learning objectives as they perform the assigned task.
3) It enables me to assess assignments quickly and yet, at the same time, to arrive at a numerical mark that accurately

reflects a student's performance with respect to these learning objectives.

4) It enables me to be more consistent in my assessment of several assignments written by students of varying ability.
5) It enables me to give every student feedback on the specific strengths and weaknesses of a completed assignment.

Some teachers might disagree with the number of performance levels I expect students to demonstrate. Why not, for example, include a fifth performance level such as a "poor" beneath the "weak"? While some teachers might find this useful, I am far more consistent in my assessment of student work when I must assign it one of only four performance levels. Forced to choose between five, I invariably award a middle-of-the-road assessment.

Other teachers might disagree with the numerical values I have attached to each performance level. For example, a student who submits an assignment that is "weak" in all four areas still receives 8 of a possible 30 points — 27% of the assignment's total value. There are two reasons for this. First, a student who achieves a "fair" assessment on each of the assessment criteria should, as a minimum, achieve a passing grade; this means that the single performance level below that should be somewhere between 0 and 50%. Since my students have already performed a number of preliminary assignments relating to this final task, they should be capable of producing work worth at least 27% of the assignment's total value; if not, I must re-examine the efficacy of the preliminary tasks I have assigned. Second, I only award 0% to students who fail to submit work. Any work, regardless of the skill with which it has been produced, deserves some value. (If, however, I feel a student has dashed off an assignment with little thought or care, I will return it and require that it be redone and submitted again with value lost for being late. Because my students have class time to collaborate in the development of their assignments, this does not occur often.)

Regarding the total possible score for each criterion, I arrive at it by focusing on the intended learning objectives and assigning the greatest value to those criteria which I have emphasized in a particular unit of study. For example, the majority of the value of the above task is determined by the student's ability to work within the confines of a particular point of view; the other criteria reflect ongoing course and school objectives regarding the presentation and mechanics of written work. In determining the total possible score for each criterion, I also examine the time each will require of a student — those requiring the most time are assigned the greatest value.

Rubrics, of course, can be as elaborate and as specific as the teacher wants, depending on the objectives of the assignment. This approach to assessing assignments does not eliminate the unexpected — I still, from time to time, find anomalies in a pile of student assignments. These, however, are usually the result of a student's being absent from class and not benefitting from the instruction and peer support I offer. If I am clear about what I expect of students and how I will translate these expectations into a final score, I increase the likelihood that my students will achieve intended learning outcomes.

As well, developing and using rubrics prevents me from arriving at an arbitrary assessment. In the past, factors such as the time of day I was marking and the location of an assignment in the pile — near the top or at the bottom — influenced my assessment of student work. This approach, however, ensures a greater degree of consistency on my part. At no time should a student ask the question "Why did Janice score a higher mark than I did?" and not receive a satisfactory answer. In fact, rubrics that focus on intended learning objectives enable students to answer such questions themselves.

8/When Process Becomes Product

As a boy, I fished almost daily along the banks of the river that meandered through my grandparents' property, catching salmon fry, speckled trout, bottom suckers, and the occasional eel that bent my fibreglass rod nearly double. Even at that young age, I understood one of the truly great mysteries of life: why catching fish is the least important part of the angling experience. There is something almost spiritual about a china-blue sky over rippling water, distant cattle sounds mingling with a symphony of frogsong and bird choirs, and a fishing line needling the river surface at acute angles. A fish on the end of that line is merely a bonus.

My daughters, on the other hand, do not share my view of this experience. Having gone fishing with me a few times each summer since they could walk, Lauren and Caitlin have yet to catch anything, much to their dismay. Out of desperation, two years ago I even took them to a nearby U-Fish where people pulled trout out of a stocked pond with almost metronomic regularity. My girls, however, stood on the bank and watched helplessly as fat, foot-long fish swam leisurely past their bait and seized the hooks of people on either side of them. On the way home, her voice thick with disgust, eight-year-old Lauren suggested we stop at Save-Easy and buy a fish from the frozen food section so we'd "at least have *something* to take home."

While I admit the U-Fish experience was somewhat less than spiritual, I am hoping my daughters will one day appreciate the *process* of fishing as well as its *result*. It is for a similar reason that I reflect in my assessment of students their involvement in the *process* of learning as well as the *results* of that learning as I discussed in Chapters 6 and 7. Sometimes, however, I consider the process to be the product.

Process as Product

In the second grade this year, Caitlin is already recognizing the importance of the process in learning. Doing homework at the dining-room table the other day, she was painstakingly printing a description of a change she would like to make in the world — one I suspected involved the eradication of green vegetables from the planet — and I saw her suddenly draw lines through half of what she'd written. Noticing the surprise on my face, she said matter-of-factly, "Our teacher told us not to fall in love with our first draft." And she doesn't. Both she and her sister recognize the value of note-jotting, organizing thoughts, trying out ideas. In assigning projects as assessment mechanisms that will receive a numerical value, I also build into that assessment opportunities to award students value for the process that culminates in that project.

First, I again need to make clear my distinction between exploratory assignments — the short tasks I give students during class and for homework — and those assignments I assess according to predetermined criteria. The latter, which I call "projects," require more than one class or evening to complete; they are the assessment tools I design that encourage students to draw together what they have learned about a particular concept, recognize its relationship to other situations and, in many cases, create a work that reflects this understanding.

The advantage of using projects as mechanisms for assessment is that they allow me to assess learning as a collaborative activity. While much of the work students do for me outside my classroom requires individual effort, many of the tasks they perform within my classroom are done in pairs and small groups. If I intend to be fair in determining the extent of student achievement of selected objectives, I cannot ignore the fact that students work together much of the time to achieve those objectives. In their assessment of beginning drivers, for example, examiners do not require motorists to parallel-park eighteen-wheelers in order to earn their drivers' licenses — they are assessed in the vehicle they learned to drive. Therefore, while I *do* test students as individuals and assign them projects as individuals, I also assess them as a community of learners involved in a process. Two ways I do this are through collaborative test situations and group projects (see Chapters 9 and 10 for further discussion of these assessment tools), but the homework/classwork record system outlined in Chapter 6 also allows me to design individual student projects that are assessed wholly in terms of the process by which the student performs them.

Combining Process and Product Assessment: The Reader's Log

Process assessment — assessing a student's involvement in the business of learning — can be achieved in many ways, all of them dependent upon the objectives the teacher intends her students to accomplish. In math and science, for example, process can be assessed through the keeping of learning logs in which students record the concepts they encounter and their understanding of them. Notes jotted about *how* a student solved a problem — or, for that matter, notes about what he did that did *not* result in a solution — are important documents of the learning process that both teacher and student can use to determine strengths and weaknesses in understanding. In physical education, students can keep fitness logs that detail physical activity and resulting physiological effects (pulse rate, respiration, etc.). In social studies, students can keep media logs in which they attach copies (or summaries) of news articles related to course content — along with responses to those articles — which can be used in a culminating project. In language arts, students can keep reading logs in which they record their responses to novels, short stories, poems, essays, films, etc., responses that can help them make important connections between form and idea.

Besides the homework/classwork assessment scheme I described in Chapter 6, the reader's log is the tool I have used most often and most successfully to assess the process of a student's learning. Although I have used it primarily in language arts instruction, it can be modified to suit the purposes of teachers in other subject areas. Adapted from reading strategies devised by Nancie Atwell, the following materials explain the reader's log as I have used it, presented in the form my junior high students received it. I have also adapted it for use with senior high students.

Interesting things happen in the mind of a reader. First of all, the mind has to "translate" the black marks on the page (called letters and words) into some sort of meaning which the reader understands. However, that isn't the only thing that happens as a reader reads. A READER'S LOG is a tool that can help a reader better understand the process of reading.

Your READER'S LOG will be a record of the thinking you do *before* you read, *while* you read, and *after* you've finished reading. There are many purposes for keeping a READER'S LOG, but the following are two important ones:

1) it forces you to think about what it is you are reading, and
2) it provides a reading record you can use to complete other work *and* to prepare for tests and exams.

How to keep a READER'S LOG:
Place several sheets of looseleaf in a duotang and write READER'S LOG and your name and class on the front cover. Place this "READER'S LOG" handout at the beginning of your duotang so you will be able to check it from time to time. When you are responding to your reading, write ONLY on the right side of the page (the side with the holes on the left). Write on every line, but skip a line between each entry. Each time you begin an entry, write the title of the story or poem or essay on a separate line and write the date in the right margin.

When to write in your READER'S LOG:
Write in your log BEFORE you begin reading, WHILE you are reading, and AFTER you have finished reading. You may not feel like writing in it WHILE you are reading, but this is often the best time because ideas and thoughts are fresh in your mind. Feel free to jot down only a few words while you are reading. Later, you might go back and write more about what you jotted down.

What to write about in your READER'S LOG:
You are free to write whatever thoughts and feelings you have about the story/poem/book/essay/article you are reading, even negative comments if you find you are not enjoying what you are reading. However, if you are not sure what to write about, the following is a list of *suggestions*. (Remember, they are given only as a guide — you may think of other things to write about.)

1) Look at the author's name. Do you remember reading anything else by this same author? If so, what was it called and what did you think of it?

2) Look at the title of the story or poem or book or essay you will be reading. What does it make you think of? Can you guess what it will be about?

3) Look at the way it has been arranged. Is it divided into separate sections or not? Does it look any different than any other stories or poems or books or essays you have seen or read?

WHILE YOU ARE READING:

4) Identify the people you are reading about and tell what you have learned about them. Write the number of the page where each person first appears.

5) Jot down anything you notice about the way the author writes. For example:

— does the author use any details that really stand out in your mind?
— does the author use a lot of dialogue (people speaking)?
— does the author include a lot of people's thoughts?
— whom does the author use to tell the story?
— does the author repeat anything?
— does the author use a flashback?
— does the author change the setting (time and place) of his story?

6) Jot down words you think are interesting or important. Copy the sentences they are used in and give the page number of each sentence.

7) Jot down things you are wondering about (things you might like to ask the author if he or she were there).

8) If you are reading a book or long story, make predictions about what will happen later and give reasons for your predictions.

AFTER YOU HAVE FINISHED READING:

9) Try summarizing in one or two sentences the main idea of what you have read.

10) Was anything different at the end than at the beginning? (Did anything change?)

11) Did anything surprise you? Explain why you were or were not surprised.

12) Jot down questions about what you have read (things you did not understand).

13) Describe how the book/story/poem/essay/article made you feel. Then tell why it made you feel that way.
14) Describe what the book/story/poem/essay/article made you think about. Did it remind you of anything you had experienced or read about before?

How your READER'S LOG will be assessed:
Your READER'S LOG will be assessed according to the effort you put into keeping it. The more you write in it, the greater the value you will receive. Check each reading assignment sheet to find out how much you need to write and how much the assignment is worth.

The following is the first of several reading assignments my students performed, this one given at the beginning of a short story unit. In class, we read, discussed, and wrote about short stories I had selected from a variety of sources. I designed "Reading Assignment #1" as a means of exposing the students to an even wider variety of stories and as an opportunity for them to relate the ideas and concepts we discussed in class to other stories and writers.

READING ASSIGNMENT #1

The following is a list of twenty short stories found in your *Crossings* textbook. After each of them is the page number where it begins and the number of pages it covers in the textbook (not including illustrations).

STORY	PAGE	TOTAL NUMBER OF PAGES
"After Twenty Years"	9	4
"The Soul of Caliban"	32	10
"The Sniper"	55	3
"Home"	62	2
"How Much Land Does a Man Need"	66	5
"Geralde and the Green, Green Grass"	73	5
"The Necklace"	80	8
"The Tell-Tale Heart"	91	5
"Goliath"	99	5
"Another Solution"	106	4
"The Lighthouse of Ste. Julie"	112	12

STORY	PAGE	TOTAL NUMBER OF PAGES
"Four Men and a Box"	169	5
"Side Bet"	179	9
"The Conjurer's Revenge"	277	2
"Through the Tunnel"	349	9
"Carpet of Roses"	372	5
"The Raft"	385	5
"Searching for Summer"	393	8
"The Half-Husky (1)"	420	8
"The Half-Husky (2)"	430	6

TOTAL: 120 pages

Assignment: Choose several of the stories listed above, read them,and record your thoughts and reactions in your READER'S LOG. You must write at least 100 words about every story you read.

How many stories do you have to read?
I don't like to assign students to read a certain number of stories because some people will choose the shortest stories. Instead, I want you to read stories that interest you; I am assigning you to read at least 60 textbook pages. Each time you read a story and write about it in your READER'S LOG, check it off the list above and keep a total of the number of pages you have read.

How much is this assignment worth?
Remember, I assess READER'S LOGS according to the effort students put into them. Students who read 60 textbook pages and write 100 words about each story will receive 24 out of 30 points. Students who read more and write more in their READER'S LOGS will receive greater value. Those who do less than this will receive less value.

When is the assignment due?
Please pass in your assignment at the beginning of class on
_____.

Not only is the reader's log useful for independent reading assignments, it is also effective when used in conjunction with specific reading tasks. In class, students benefit from sharing their responses to the same story or article or poem because different students notice different things in their reading by virtue of the fact that each brings different experiences, both as a reader and as a human being, to a text. Out of class, I can quickly check to see that students are doing the reading (i.e., are involving themselves in the business of learning) and note some of the responses I might wish to draw upon later in our study.

With regard to the assessment of these reader's log assignments, I regularly read and respond to my students' log entries and, in the process, I record the amount they read and write.

Portfolio Assessment

At ten years of age, Lauren is only four inches shorter than her mother. Caitlin, on the other hand, is small for her eight years, a fact that friends and family members comment on frequently — much to Caitlin's dismay. It's tough being the smallest person in her family/class/art group/etc., but it's even tougher being reminded of it all the time. Sometimes when she needs to "feel bigger," she and I take out the photo albums and pore over the hundreds of pictures my wife and I have taken since our children were born — it's only when she sees how small she used to be that Caitlin is able to appreciate how much she's really grown after all.

It is for this reason that portfolio assessment makes so much sense, particularly with regard to language arts. Rather than looking at a single example of a student's work produced at a single point in time, a teacher (not to mention the student herself, her parents, other teachers, and so on) can get a much clearer sense of her achievement by looking at a number of such examples produced over a period of time: a month, a term, a year, even several years. There are several books available that describe portfolio assessment, and Nancie Atwell's *In the Middle: Reading, Writing, and Learning with Adolescents* remains one of the best in its explanation of assessment in the areas of writing and reading. In it, Atwell describes how she individualizes instruction as well as assessment by helping — through brief conferences — each student set goals for himself and then, after a period of time, determining with that student — again in conference — the extent to which he has met those goals. Besides making it very clear to the student the learning objectives he will focus on during a particular period of time, this approach makes the student an integral part of the assessment process, allowing him the opportunity to reflect upon his efforts to achieve those objectives and, if necessary, to defend his assessment of his success in accomplishing them. Surely, this is teaching and learning at their best.

Often, however, the conference approach to portfolio assessment becomes an ideal that is inaccessible in traditional secondary school settings. Teachers facing more than 130 students every day may find it difficult to confer effectively with them in the limited time available. Also, so much of the success of this method depends on personal teaching style — specifically, the rapport and climate of trust the individual teacher is able to establish in her classroom. However, portfolio assessment is still possible when teachers consider the following questions with respect to assessing work over time:

1) What part will the portfolio play in my overall evaluation of student achievement?
2) What indicators will I use to determine student achievement in my assessment of portfolios?

There are many ways teachers can incorporate portfolio assessment into an overall evaluation mechanism. The best way, of course, is to make certain all involved understand the structure of this. While I am talking primarily about language arts, the process by which I arrived at a scheme for assessing writing portfolios would be similar to the process one might go through in assessing portfolios in other courses.

In deciding how I would structure my language arts course and what it was I would require my students to achieve, I knew that I wanted to give the students the opportunity to write pieces of their own choosing. Yes, there were specific forms of writing I wanted them to try, but I also wanted them to have the opportunity to attempt others they were interested in and to be rewarded for these attempts. The following is the mechanism I developed to assess my students' participation in writing workshops every Friday:

NAME: _____ CLASS: _____ DATE: _____					
WRITING WORKSHOP ASSESSMENT:	POOR	WEAK	FAIR	STRONG	OUTSTANDING
1. My commitment to making the workshop work for me: a) How much writing have I done?	0	2	4	6	7
b) Have I met the goals I set for myself?	0	2	4	6	7
2. My commitment to making the workshop work for others: a) Have I participated effectively in writers' conferences?	0	2	4	6	7
b) Have I participated during sharing time?	0	2	4	6	7

TOTAL SCORE: _____
28

In previous rubrics, I included only four performance levels. Because I designed this rubric for student use, I included a fifth level — "poor" — to reflect non-performance in a particular area. For example, a student who, during the course of the term, chose not to confer with others would receive no value for this portion of the assessment.

At the beginning of the school year, I discussed with my students the goals of the workshop and gave them a copy of the above form so they would understand how I would assess their performance in it. Then I explained how I would monitor their participation using the following form, a variation of Nancie Atwell's "status of the class" record:

Like Atwell, I spent the first four to five minutes of every workshop recording what students were working on, then allowed them to work independently or with others. I encouraged students to confer with me as well as with each other on the pieces they were writing, and I recorded when this happened. Finally, I recorded if students shared during the final eight to ten minutes of the workshop; the purpose of the sharing time was for students to hear what others were working on

WORKPLAN = what the student plans to work on
C = confers effectively with others on a piece of writing
P = participates in sharing time

DATE	Sept. 11	C	P	Sept. 18	C	P	Sept. 25	C	P
	WORKPLAN	C	P	WORKPLAN	C	P	WORKPLAN	C	P
Melanie A.	Collecting info for "Summer"			Draft 1 of "Summer"		✓	Revise D.1 "Summer"	✓	
Richard C.	Draft 1 of "Brother"	✓		Draft 1 of "Brother"			Draft 1 of "Brother"		
Trevor E.	Choosing a topic			Collecting infor for "Soccer"			Drafting leads for "Soccer"		

as well as to recognize that others experience similar problems in their writing.

Before the end of each reporting term, I asked students to assess their own performance based on the criteria provided, and I encouraged them to write notes accompanying their assessments if they felt I might overlook an important achievement. When these were submitted, I referred to my records of the students' work as well as their writing files to see if these reflected their self-assessments. If there were discrepancies — in fact, students most often assessed themselves lower than I would have — I spoke with those students and together we arrived at a mark that was more equitable.

Some Final Thoughts about Portfolio Assessment

One of the advantages of portfolio assessment is that it requires students to reflect on a body of work in terms of goals they have set for themselves. For example, if a student has identified as a goal the finishing of at least one narrative or the trying of a variety of forms of writing or the use of concrete details to make writing show rather than tell, she can examine the body of work to find evidence of having worked toward accomplishing this goal. In this way, students become responsible not only for their own assessment but for the learning that precedes that assessment as well. Also, students have the opportunity to recognize growth over time as a measure of success rather than individual performance on an isolated task. Finally, portfolio development and assessment can be tailored to the specific needs of each student, allowing for students of greater ability to work toward more advanced goals while others can concentrate on improving particular areas of weakness.

There are, however, concerns regarding portfolios which teachers need to address if they choose to make them a part of their instructional and assessment schemes. First, portfolios are time-consuming; the teacher must carefully plan the class time to be allotted for students to work on their portfolios and to confer with the teacher regarding eventual assessment. Also, students unfamiliar with this form of assessment need to be trained in all the areas in which they will be assessed. I could not, for example, assess my students on the frequency of their writing conferences or their participation in sharing time until I had modeled these activities and made them fully aware of what I expected. Finally, space is a consideration. It is best if portfolios are kept in one area so student work is not lost or damaged; however, creating a place to which 130 students can have access and still not interfere with the teacher's own files may be difficult. (I have used cardboard boxes filled with homemade bristol board dividers labeled with letters; in these boxes, students filed their folders according to their last initial.)

While these are very real concerns, the benefits offered by portfolio assessment are considerable. Just as Caitlin takes pleasure in seeing how much she has grown by looking at how small she used to be, students take pride in achieving specific goals over time.

9/Behavioural Assessment

MELISSA: So what did you think?

SCOTT: I liked it.

TANYA: Me, too.

JEREMY: Yeah.

MELISSA: Any suggestions? Like, what I could do to make it better?

(Silence. SCOTT shifts in his seat. TANYA coughs.)

JEREMY: There were parts in your story where you could have, you know, included more details.

MELISSA: Like where?

JEREMY: Um — the part where you and your mother argue about cleaning your room.

TANYA: My mom is always after me to clean mine.

SCOTT: Mine, too.

JEREMY: You should see my room. Whew! (Laughs)

MELISSA: My room isn't always that bad.

TANYA: Oh yeah? What about that time we got pizza all over your bedspread?

SCOTT: Gross!

JEREMY: You think that's gross, one time my brother and me...

And so it goes.

The conversation above is typical of the interaction groups displayed in my classroom for years. Like all teachers, I knew that great things can occur when students work together effectively in small groups. However, despite my efforts to create an environment in which they could happen, they usually didn't. Despite my efforts to design activities that would encourage cooperation among group members, a familiar pattern emerged. High-achievers assigned to work with those I perceived as less capable found themselves doing most — and, in some cases, all — of the work. Class time set aside for group collaboration was often wasted by students less interested in working than in waiting for me to get out of earshot so they could talk about more important things — dances, parties, boyfriends and girlfriends. Deadlines were missed. Work that was completed was invariably inferior to what I knew my students were capable of producing.

What had gone wrong? The answer embarrassed me. For all my talk about instruction being tied to learning objectives, for all the importance I had placed on preparing students for the tasks I gave them, I had overlooked one crucial element: I had not taught my students *how* to work in groups. Although students naturally form social groups and take part in a number of group activities both in and out of school, teachers cannot assume — as I did — that students know how to work together effectively on the tasks they encounter in classrooms. Any teacher who has ever served on a school or district committee recognizes that even professional educators do not always work well together; how much more likely is it, then, that students will experience difficulty in this regard? Very likely.

I cannot begin to address all the issues associated with cooperative learning in the classroom, nor is it my intention. Many fine books have been written on the subject, some of which I have listed in Appendix D. All are excellent resources for teachers interested in learning more about the theory and practice of small-group learning.

The Problem with Groupwork at the Secondary Level

Many schools, particularly those at the elementary and middle school levels, place great emphasis on teamwork and collaboration by staff members which, in turn, carries over into classrooms. Such schools, as well, work hard to develop a strong sense of community among their students which teachers are able to draw upon as they involve students in cooperative learning activities.

Such environments, however, are not yet the norm in secondary schools. Separated by subject areas and regulated by timetables which offer little if any time for collaboration with other staff members, teachers often work in isolation, developing individual approaches to classroom management and instructional design. As a result, students often find themselves moving between several very different learning environments in a single day. Imagine how difficult it is, therefore, for students who are required to perform all tasks individually in one classroom to move to another classroom — often with different classmates — in which they are required to work cooperatively. It is little wonder that teachers at the secondary level find students reluctant or ineffective participants in group tasks.

If teachers intend to make small-group learning a part of their classroom instruction and to make student performance of group tasks a part of their overall assessment, they should be prepared to do both of the following:

1) to investigate the theory behind and the practice of small-group learning so they will better understand the dynamics of group interaction, and

2) to show students not only how to work in small groups but also why it is important to be able to do so.

Reading books such as the ones listed in Appendix D and visiting classrooms where teachers have used cooperative learning effectively are ways teachers can accomplish the first objective. The following section outlines how I accomplish the second.

Preparing Students to Work in Groups

After I have met with a class a few times and my students understand what I expect of each of them as individuals (as I outlined in Chapter 5), I spend a period helping them understand what I expect of them as members of the group — the class — they are a part of this school year. After asking who among them belongs to groups — committees, teams, etc. — in the school, I list the names of these groups on the board. Then I ask who belongs to groups outside the school and list these on the board. I continue by asking for and listing names of groups their friends or family members belong to, and so on. By the time they have finished identifying them all, I have usually filled much of the board.

Following this, I ask my students why teachers have them work in groups, and they offer a variety of reasons, not all of which are positive. One student this year, for example, responded, "So teachers won't have as much to mark." Invariably, many of them fail to recognize what working in groups has to offer them, and I ask them to consider the groups we have listed on the board: why do people belong to them? I record their suggestions — to meet people, to have fun, to learn new things, to get a job done faster, etc. — and then comment that teachers have students work in classroom groups for the same reasons. I also add, however, that groupwork allows students to learn by talking through ideas and that the ability to work in groups is a life skill as well. I demonstrate the latter by showing on the overhead projector several job ads clipped from various newspapers, each of them containing lines like "excellent interpersonal skills required" or "ability to work as a team member essential."

After demonstrating the "why" behind my use of groupwork, I ask students to describe — without using names — some positive group experiences and to identify what made those experiences positive. Most find it easier to do the second task: describe — again, without using names — some negative group experiences and identify what made those experiences negative. Invariably, the reasons for group experiences being either positive or negative have less to do with the task the group faces than with the people working in the group.

Extending this idea, I have six volunteers come to the front of the room and read a transcript of a group trying to solve a problem assigned by their teacher. (Some teachers show videos of groups at work, but I prefer the role-playing scenario because many students enjoy performing, especially when given the chance to perform inappropriate behaviours.) Each performer wears a placard bearing the name of a group member, and together they read the scene — only three to four minutes long — twice. During the first reading, I ask the rest of the class to record on one side of a piece of paper the names of people who are being helpful, and on the other side the names of the people who are being unhelpful. The second time the scene is read, I ask the rest of the class to try to record specific behaviours that each person performs which are helpful or unhelpful.

After the performers have read twice, I ask the class to share what they have noted. The transcript I use — which may be found in *Bridges 2* (Prentice Hall) — includes people who disrupt the group's task by joking around, grandstanding, insulting others, and so on. I ask the class to suggest reasons why some people perform so inappropriately, and they usually arrive at two: these group members genuinely dislike the people they have to work with, or they don't understand how to perform the task and they behave in this manner so others won't discover their inability. Then we look at the helpful behaviours which range from organizing to encouraging to volunteering to clarifying, and I explain that, in order for a group to work effectively, its members must perform these behaviours. By doing so, they can overcome the problems of personal conflict and insecurity which often plague group interaction.

I end the class by asking the students to jot down and pass in the names of one or two classmates they would feel comfortable working with. Before they return the next day, I make up a number of groups which will stay together for the next three to four weeks. I make groups no smaller than three and no larger than five and, along with pairing each student with one classmate they would like to work with, I try to achieve a heterogeneous mix of ability and sex.

The following class, I review briefly the helpful behaviours the students identified the previous day and pass out the following sheet which they place in a special section of their binder where they can refer to it often in the months ahead. Adapted from materials I have encountered in cooperative workshops, it outlines specific behaviours that contribute to successful group interaction.

GROUP ROLES: HELPFUL BEHAVIOURS AND WHAT THEY LOOK LIKE

In any group, people perform a number of roles. For example, everyone should be a PARTICIPATOR, a person who freely offers ideas and suggestions AND volunteers for particular duties. However, there are other roles that need to be performed if a group is to work effectively. One group member may perform more than one of these roles during a group session.

ROLE   BEHAVIOUR

LEADER
1) gets things started
2) organizes duties
3) reminds group members of responsibilities (keeps everyone on task)
4) identifies problems the group is having

CLARIFIER	1) makes sure everyone understands
	2) asks group members for more information about their ideas
	3) sums up what was said or done
ENCOURAGER	1) listens carefully to group members (watches faces of people talking, smiles, nods, etc.)
	2) encourages group members to participate
	3) praises group members
CHECKER	1) checks to see if group members agree
	2) checks to see if everyone has seen/heard
	3) watches the time

I explain that each time the students get into a group, I will require that they turn to this paper and select a group role and perform the behaviours associated with it. No one should perform the same group role all the time — everyone should take turns being the leader, clarifier, encourager, and checker. I tell them that, in the beginning, I will assess groupwork only on the basis of whether group members perform their roles. As they become more comfortable with their groups, I will assess them according to other criteria, but a component of their mark will always be determined by my observations of their group behaviours.

To give them practice in performing these roles as well as some understanding of how I will observe them, I have them take part in a "fishbowl" exercise in which I pair the groups, one of which performs a group activity while the other group, seated around the first, records the behaviours demonstrated. To do this, the members of the observing group each select a different individual to watch, and they check off on the following sheet, also adapted from teacher workshop materials, the various behaviours they see demonstrated, one checkmark each time they see it. I read the sheet aloud beforehand to familiarize them with the various behaviours and, while I do not expect them to be able to record everything they see, I tell them to do their best.

Name: _____ Class:_____

The following is a list of helpful and unhelpful behaviours that can occur during group work. To make you more aware of these behaviours, you are assigned to watch and listen to _____ as he/she works in a group. Each time he/she says or does something you see listed below, put a checkmark to the right of that behaviour. (If you see the same behaviour eight times, put eight checkmarks beside it.) When the group has finished, you will be asked to share your checklist with the person you observed.

HELPFUL BEHAVIOURS:

Gets things going:
1) helps to start the discussion   _____
2) helps group members choose
   particular duties   _____
Clarifies:
3) asks group members for more information about their ideas   _____
Contributes:
4) offers ideas, suggestions,
   opinions   _____
5) volunteers for particular duties   _____
Draws ideas together:
6) checks to see if group members
   agree   _____
7) explores how an idea might work   _____
8) sums up what has been said   _____
Encourages:
9) listens carefully to what is
   happening   _____
10) smiles or nods in encouragement   _____
11) encourages other group members
    to contribute   _____
Keeps on track:
12) reminds the group members of
    their purpose   _____
13) lets members know how well
    they are doing to achieve their
    purpose   _____
14) identifies things that block the
    group's progress   _____

Competes:
15) tries to boss other members of
    the group   _____
Blocks:
16) does not listen to what others are
    saying   _____
17) puts down group members   _____
18) puts down the teacher or
    assignment   _____
Horses around:
19) jokes or makes fun of others   _____
Withdraws:
20) is silent or does other work   _____

Because students are uncomfortable being observed, especially by other students, I give each inner group an activity for which there are no correct answers; often, in fact, it is not specifically related to the course I am teaching them. In the past, for example, I have asked groups to invent a game that could be played by four people trapped in an elevator, to suggest uses for a strange-looking object, to attempt to solve a murder given a list of clues, and so on, the purpose being to enable students to focus on practicing group behaviours rather than on mastering course content. Regardless of the activity, I require each group to pass in a record of what it has accomplished, something I do throughout the year to demonstrate that groups are accountable for the time they spend together.

Following this exercise, which usually takes about fifteen minutes, I ask the outer group members to share what they recorded with the people they were observing. Then, as a whole class, they share and discuss their reactions to the exercise. Before the class ends, I ask each student to record on the back of her "Group Roles" sheet one or two things she needs to improve when working in her group next time.

The next class is a repeat of this one, except that the activity is different and the groups that were observed last day now do the observing.

Assessing Group Behaviours

In the first two weeks following the "fishbowl" exercise, I ease my students into groupwork by having them work in pairs on short (five- to ten-minute) tasks, then longer tasks. The purpose here is to create a "comfort zone" — which is especially important for students unaccustomed to working cooperatively — and, at the same time, to give students a chance to practice helpful behaviours. Following this, they move into the larger groups in which they will work for the next four weeks.

It is at this point that I raise the issue of accountability within each group. I explain that in the weeks ahead I will assess their efforts to work cooperatively with each other; whenever they move into their groups to perform a task, I will move about the room offering help but, at the same time, I will be observing the way they interact and I will record in my binder beside each person's name an S if I see him performing helpful behaviours, a U if I see both helpful and unhelpful behaviours, and an X if I see only unhelpful behaviours demonstrated. If I see all members of a group working together effectively, I will record a bonus mark (+) beside each group member's name. This record will become part of the homework/classwork record which I described in Chapter 6.

Some students immediately question whether such an assessment is fair; after all, if they had difficulty observing a single student during the fishbowl activity, how can I accurately observe all students working in all groups? The answer, of course, is simple: I can't. I will be able to observe each person only briefly each time they are working in groups, and, since they will not always know when I am observing them, it is important that group members always practice the roles they have selected.

My students do not work in groups every class, but each time they do, I look for evidence of students working effectively: sitting close together, watching the faces of people talking, asking questions, and so on. When I see these behaviours, I may interrupt the class and call attention to them, praising the people involved; if I don't wish to interrupt their work, I make a note and comment on these observations toward the end of the period. The more I do this, the better my students understand what I expect of them.

10 / Assessing Tests and Examinations

"You may begin."

There are few directions that teachers give in their classrooms which create as much anxiety in students as those final words prior to the writing of a test or examination. Unfortunately, it was not until I returned to university to study for my master's degree that I realized the extent to which this was true. Only one of the twelve courses I took required the writing of a timed, closed-book examination, but this single experience helped me to appreciate what it is I do to students each time I give a test. While the examination I wrote was worth only 10% of my final mark in that course, I worried for days about having to write it.

Imagine, then, the effect tests and examinations have on students who are not comfortable with course material, who must do well because the test is worth a considerable percentage of the term, and who have no clear idea how to prepare for it in the first place. While I certainly did not enjoy writing the exam for that master's course, I am grateful to the instructor who required it because I have not given a test or examination since then without recalling that experience.

Pros and Cons of Tests/Examinations

Teachers give tests and examinations for a number of reasons, the most common being to determine the extent to which students have mastered course content and skills. One of the best arguments in support of these assessment tools is that they require students to consolidate learning: in looking back over a unit or a term in preparation for a test or examination, students are able to make connections between topics which previously might have appeared fragmented.

The appeal tests and examinations have for educators is that they offer teachers a degree of control over the assessment situation which out-of-class assignments do not, and they ensure — supposedly — that the student actually knows what it is she is supposed to know and is not merely copying the work of others. As well, since most tests and examinations are completed in a single sitting, the volume of work which teachers must assess is far less than the work associated with lengthier assignments, projects, and so on. However, these advantages also embody the greatest weaknesses inherent in tests and examinations as tools for assessment.

First, as teachers meet a student population that is increasingly varied in ability and background, many recognize the need to structure learning situations that will encourage cooperation and collaboration among participants. Few of society's problems exist in isolation, and it is only through the cooperation of many people that solutions to major problems are found. If schools exist to promote the development of effective citizens, learning situations should be structured to encourage and to facilitate this development — hence the increase in the number of secondary teachers who have adapted instructional techniques to encourage cooperative small-group learning. However, assessment practices should reflect instructional strategies — students encouraged to collaborate on the work in a unit should not be assessed solely in a manner that militates against collaboration; unfortunately, however, this is often the design of most tests and examinations.

Also, because of the single-sitting timeframe in which they are written, tests and examinations often offer students little opportunity to demonstrate more than the lowest-level cognitive abilities. Most traditional tests and examinations, for example, test students' ability to recall and to comprehend information; some, as well, test their ability to apply this understanding to new situations. Fewer, however, require students to perform the higher-level tasks of analysis, synthesis, and evaluation because the time required for experimentation and reflection — which must accompany such processes — is not available. And, of course, fewer still allow students to demonstrate learning in the affective and psychomotor domains.

While the debate over the educational value of tests and, in particular, examinations continues, it is likely that most secondary teachers are required to include them in their assessment practices. As a result, it is necessary for teachers to design tests and examinations that assess student performance accurately and fairly.

Designing Tests/Examinations

Once a teacher has decided to use a test to assess student mastery of course objectives, he must determine how this mastery can be demonstrated. Obviously, true-or-false, multiple-choice, and fill-in-the-blank questions offer two advantages: they allow objective assessment of student knowledge, and they require little time to score. The disadvantage of such test items is that they focus on low-level content recall and they encourage the perception that learning is the memorization of facts. Also, since they require students to write only single words or — in the case of multiple-choice questions — single letters, they reduce the importance of writing as a means of communicating understanding.

Test questions that require students to write longer answers — paragraphs or essays — are more time-consuming to assess and require much more subjectivity on the part of teachers who must mark them. However, they allow students to demonstrate more clearly what they know or are able to do, and they require students to use writing to convey understanding, formulating and organizing ideas and presenting them in a meaningful manner.

I am sure there are few language arts teachers who have not been asked the following questions by other faculty members: "Don't you teach kids how to spell anymore?" "Don't you teach kids how to write complete sentences anymore?" "Don't you teach kids how to write paragraphs anymore?" Although usually offered in good humour, such questions suggest that many secondary teachers view their role as purveyors of subject content and it is the sole duty of language arts teachers to teach students writing skills which should transfer to all subject areas.

Much more has been written about the "language across the curriculum" debate than I could begin to include here, but I believe if teachers are to assess students on the basis of any criterion, that criterion must be a part of the instruction students receive in their courses. Merely telling students that a portion of their mark will be based on mechanics and writing style does not constitute writing instruction. There is considerable disagreement even among language arts teachers concerning the hallmarks of "good" writing — just ask any secondary student who has had more than one English teacher. Consequently, it is unrealistic — even counterproductive — for a teacher to assess the quality of students' writing without first having those students understand the standards by which their writing will be assessed.

"I don't have time to teach my students how to write. I don't have enough time to teach them the curriculum as it is." I understand this argument, and I appreciate it. There are growing demands on instructional time, and teachers see added instructional tasks as impossible to achieve. There are ways to address this problem, and I discuss some of these in Chapter 11. If, however, a teacher cannot commit class time to writing instruction, no part of his assessment of his students' work should be based on this criterion.

"What about spelling? Surely I can expect my students to spell correctly, can't I?" Many teachers do expect their students to spell correctly, but how many adults — teachers included — spell perfectly? I consider myself a better-than-average speller, but I consult a dictionary for words I seldom use. If I am going to expect students to spell correctly — particularly those words specific to my discipline — then I must first identify those words I want them to spell correctly and offer strategies for remembering their spelling. Failing this, I should offer instruction in the use of dictionaries and allow my students access to them during tests.

"Isn't this going too far? What about standards? What about simple expectations for acceptable work?" This is a good point. However, until a school agrees on what these standards are and how their achievement will be assessed across the curriculum, individual teachers must address the problem in their own classrooms. In my case, I go over sample responses to test questions with the whole class, using rubrics such as the following one I designed to help students to identify strengths and weaknesses in opinion papers prior to their writing a test that required similar responses.

By examining, discussing and ranking a number of sample test responses in light of these criteria, students are better able to understand what comprises a successful discussion of opinion and, subsequently, are better able to write one when required to do so on a test.

The writer states his/her opinion clearly.	WEAK	FAIR	STRONG	OUTSTANDING
The writer uses reasons and examples to support this opinion.	WEAK	FAIR	STRONG	OUTSTANDING
The writer explains all his/her ideas fully and does not expect the reader to know what he/she means.	WEAK	FAIR	STRONG	OUTSTANDING
The writer includes only ideas andinformation that support his/her opinion (nothing is extra).	WEAK	FAIR	STRONG	OUTSTANDING
The writer arranges his/her ideas in a logical order that is easy to follow.	WEAK	FAIR	STRONG	OUTSTANDING
The writer has edited carefully for the mechanical errors we have studied.	WEAK	FAIR	STRONG	OUTSTANDING

Preparing Students for Tests/Examinations

I recall vividly a June afternoon during the 1970s as my high school classmates and I sat waiting for our English examination to begin. A ripple of movement and muted expressions of astonishment punctuated the quiet as students turned over their exam papers and found a single question: "Explain the difference between a grape and an elephant."

One other thing I recall vividly about the experience was the low mark I scored. Because our teacher was an unorthodox individual who, throughout the year, had strayed considerably from the syllabus and had stressed creative writing over all other forms, I assumed the question was intended to evoke a highly imaginative response; accordingly, I launched into a colourful narrative in which a warrior embarked on a great quest for two items he had never before seen: a grape and an elephant. My response scored a barely passing grade because our teacher, as it turned out, wanted us to respond in an expository mode.

Every year I share that experience with my own students to underscore what I consider to be the most important tenet of test-taking: a test or examination should never be a surprise to a student. If it is, someone has not done his job: either the student has not prepared sufficiently for it, or the teacher has not prepared his student for it. While the former involves a number of issues beyond the scope of this book, the latter is something I intend to address here. There are many things teachers can do to prepare students for tests and examinations, especially those that are worth a considerable percentage of the term mark:

1) Teach students test-taking strategies which can help eliminate or minimize the stress often associated with the experience. Strategies my students find helpful, for example, are jotting down brief notes (formulas, terms, etc.) on the back of the test paper before reading the test, doing the easiest questions first, briefly planning an answer before attempting a first draft, and so on.

2) Make sure students have a clear idea what they are to learn in every class. Most teachers tell their students at the beginning of each class what they will be focusing on that period. I write this on the board in the form of lesson objectives which I have my students copy in their binders as soon as they enter my classroom. I do this for three reasons. First, copying the lesson objectives alerts the students to what it is I want them to learn that day and helps them focus on the purpose of the activities I have prepared for them. Second, it is an effective classroom management technique which ensures that my students settle down to work immediately. Finally, because they are written as performance objectives (for example, "Use a compass to bisect an angle" or "Identify elements of bias in a piece of writing"), these lesson objectives become a record of all the things I expect my students to be able to do in the course of a unit. In preparing for a test, they look back over these objectives and make sure they can perform each of the tasks they have listed. If they can't, they should see me or their classmates for extra help prior to the test.

3) Give example questions which have appeared on tests in previous years and have students discuss how they might answer them.
4) Give students examples of student responses to previous test questions and have students rank them from most to least successful. Subsequent discussion of these rankings alerts students to the criteria that determine effective responses.
5) Have students work in small groups to design their own test for a particular unit of work. Not only does this help them anticipate the sorts of tasks I might ask them to perform on a test, it also serves as an effective mechanism for review because it requires students to reflect on the entire unit and identify particular areas of importance. On several occasions, I have created a unit test using one or two items developed by each group, thereby giving them input into the assessment mechanism.
6) Give quizzes to help students focus on particular course objectives and the means by which their understanding of those objectives will be assessed. Quizzes are less threatening than tests because they encompass less course material and usually have far less impact on a student's overall mark than the value received on a test. However, if a teacher is going to use quizzes as a means of assessing student performance, she must ensure that her students understand at the beginning of the course what part they will play in their assessment.

Some Suggestions for Creating Tests/Examinations

Several years ago, I attended an in-service on assessment practices at which a presenter berated teachers who made up tests at the end of a unit. "Tests should be constructed before a unit begins," he said. "Teachers who scurry around making up a test at the last minute haven't done their job."

I understand his reasoning: he felt that the task of creating a test at the beginning of a unit allows — perhaps forces — the teacher to focus on the specific learning objectives she wants her students to achieve, and, in turn, these objectives should guide the instruction the teacher will provide throughout the unit. As I have emphasized throughout this book, I agree that the planning of specific learning objectives should precede everything else a teacher does. However, I believe that this can be accomplished without the actual designing of the test that will serve as the assessment mechanism.

There are two reasons why I feel it is advantageous to create a test at the end of a unit rather than at the beginning. First, whatever value is assigned to a test question should reflect the relative amount of time which students spend learning the concept involved in the question. How will a teacher know what concepts she has spent most of her class time teaching until she has taught those concepts? Second, during the course of a unit, students often connect with ideas that are of particular interest to them, and teachers can choose to capitalize on those interests. I mentioned in a previous chapter that, during a social studies unit I taught on immigration in the 1800s, one of my students brought in a book of political cartoons which reflected some of the issues associated with immigrants and immigration during that time period. The class enjoyed discussing several of the cartoons, recognizing the importance of prior knowledge on the part of the reader in heightening the reader's appreciation of a cartoonist's humour and message. This eventually led us to look for information that would help clarify the intent of cartoons whose messages were not readily apparent, and this, in turn, led to a question I eventually included on their unit test: providing copies of several political cartoons from the period, I asked my students to describe the issue addressed in one cartoon and to identify the cartoonist's purpose in presenting the issue in this manner. This question would never have appeared if I had created the unit test at the beginning of the unit.

Besides allowing student input to shape a test during the course of a unit, I have found the following suggestions helpful in designing the test itself:

1) Time your test. Besides allotting greater value to questions based on concepts students spend the longest time on in class, I also assign value to questions based on the amount of time students will take to answer them during the test period. Whenever possible, I follow a general rule of thumb: for every minute I expect it will take a student to complete a question, I assign one point. Thus, if a question takes 4-5 minutes to complete, it will be worth half the value of a question that will take 8-10 minutes to complete. It is

important for the teacher to try writing the test himself before giving it to his students because this will help him determine whether he has allowed sufficient time for them to answer the questions satisfactorily.

2) *Include point values for each question.* I make sure I include the total value of the test at the top of the test paper and the value of each question in the margin beside the question. In this way, students can decide how much time they should spend on a particular question. For example, if a question is only worth 3 of a total 45 points, a student should not take 15 minutes of a 45-minute test period to answer it.

3) *State directions clearly.* I determine specific instructions students should keep in mind when writing a particular test, and I go over these in classes prior to the test. I also list them at the top of the test paper to remind students what I expect. For example, the following directions appeared on a recent math test:
   1) Work neatly in pencil.
   2) Do all work on this test paper in the spaces provided.
   3) You may use a calculator, but be sure to show your work.
   4) Draw diagrams wherever possible.
   5) Write answers to problems in complete sentences.

The importance of such directions is that they identify specific performance expectations which I will consider in my assessment of my students' work. For example, if a student uses a calculator without including the work which demonstrates how she arrived at specific answers, she will receive little value for correct answers.

4) *Ensure that materials are legible.* If students must work with specific materials to answer a test question, these materials should be clear and easily read. For example, if students must read and respond to an article or examine and draw conclusions from a diagram, that article or diagram should be completely legible. I have seen tests and examinations that included materials that were almost impossible to decipher; if I experienced such difficulty, I can only imagine the problems these materials created for the students whose assessment was determined by their response to them.

5) *Phrase questions and problems carefully.* I need to make sure that the test items I design elicit the responses I intend. I've often heard students complain "You know what I meant" after I've given them little value for a test answer that offers only cursory discussion of a concept. "Yes," I respond, "I know what you meant, but I'm not assessing you on what I *assume* you can do." One way to avoid this is to provide students with a specific context in which to respond to a question. For example, during a math unit on measurement, my eighth-graders had difficulty putting into words their understanding of the concepts of area and volume. I knew that, at the end of the unit, I wanted to determine how well they had understood the distinction, but I also did not want them to assume I "knew what they meant." Therefore, I created the following test question: "Ben is six years old and does not understand the difference between area and volume. Explain what these terms mean so that Ben will understand them."

One of my favourite "Peanuts" cartoons shows Peppermint Patti looking at a test paper on which is written, "Explain World War II." Just as students should not expect a teacher to "know what they mean" by a vague test answer, I cannot assume that my students know what I mean by a vague test question — I must find the clearest possible way of phrasing each item.

The best strategy I have found for designing clear test questions is to have someone else — preferably not a teacher who might "know what I mean" — read them to determine if any confusion might arise. Another strategy is to create test items two or three days in advance and read them a couple of days later — often, problems with wording become more apparent when we distance ourselves from our writing for a period of time.

6) *Assess what you have taught.* While I have already stressed the importance of assessing students only on the basis of what we teach them, it is worthwhile noting that test items are often worded in such a way that they test student performance in areas we may not even realize. For example, in the question, "Explain the significance of the white feather in the story 'Beach,'" the teacher assumes the student understands what is meant by the term "significance."

If the teacher has used the term in class and has shown how elements of a story can be viewed as "significant," this question should be straightforward for her students. If, however, the teacher has not specifically used the term in this context, she is, in effect, assessing not only her students' understanding of the literary image but her students' knowledge of the question's vocabulary as well. A more appropriate wording of the question, therefore, might be, "Explain why the white feather is important in the story 'Beach.'"

7) *Edit tests carefully.* Besides ensuring the clear wording of test questions, teachers must take care to avoid misspellings and typographical errors which will hinder a student's understanding of a question. I have seen teachers walk from class to class during a final examination clarifying problems such as these; not only does this interrupt students who may be working on other parts of the exam, but it also reduces the likelihood that all students are being assessed in the same manner. If, for example, the teacher explains the correction one way to one class -- or one student — and one way to another, the test item will, in effect, be different for each one and may evoke a different response. How, then, can a teacher assess both the same way? Therefore, just as it is important to concentrate on clear and appropriate wording of questions, it is equally important for teachers to ensure that their tests and examinations are carefully edited before giving them to their students.

8) *Arrange questions according to level of difficulty.* If I include objective questions on a test, I include these at the very beginning of the paper; those questions that require students to plan and develop longer answers appear later in the test. Of course, students are free to answer questions in whatever order they choose but, because objective questions are often less threatening than longer essay-type questions, it is helpful for students to see these first. Much of a student's success on a test or examination depends on his ability to cope with the stress of the test situation, and if he attempts these less demanding questions at the beginning, he is more likely to feel confident about his ability to complete the remainder of the test.

9) *Allow time for self-checking.* I "build into" every test and

examination time for students to check over their work. Teachers frequently require students to write multiple drafts of assignments and to revise their writing; while it may not be possible for students to write multiple drafts of test questions, students should be allotted time to check over their work. Because they must work quickly, it is common for students to misread test questions, to omit required work, and so on. Time provided for students to check over their work often permits them to identify and correct problems, thereby ensuring the teacher she is assessing a student's performance of learning objectives rather than a student's ability to work quickly in a linear fashion.

10) *Learn from your own tests.* I once had a teacher who continually reminded her students to save the tests they wrote, telling them, "You can learn just as much from a test you did poorly on as one you did well on." I now tell my own students this. However, the same advice is true for teachers — we can learn much about how to design tests from the results our own tests elicit. Each time I give a test, I discover something I need to improve next time, and, while I seldom give the same test more than once, I am able to apply this understanding to future versions of it. When I discover a problem with a test, whether it be the wording of a question or the amount of time I have allowed for students to complete a task, I attach a note to my master copy to remind me of the improvement I need to make should I have to prepare a test on a similar unit again.

Also, it is helpful to elicit student reactions to tests, either the test as a whole or individual test items. One colleague, for example, includes questions at the end of each examination which require students to comment on the exam-writing experience by identifying questions that were most/least difficult and why, describing the order they answered the questions in and why, and so on.

11) *Encourage students to challenge a mark.* While many teachers resent having to justify the marks they give students, one language arts teacher showed me the value in encouraging students to question their assessments. If a student disagrees with a mark on a test or assignment, she encourages him to challenge the mark in writing, explaining why he feels the mark is unfair, identifying the

value he believes the test answer or assignment should receive, and demonstrating why it should receive this value. This practice has several positive results. First, it encourages students to be more critical of their own work; forced to justify a higher mark for her answer, a student must recognize both the merits and shortcomings of that answer. Second, although teachers should strive for consistency in assessment, all are human and capable of inconsistency from time to time; therefore, a student may be able to identify merits which the teacher has overlooked in her initial assessment. Finally, it allows students to use writing for a real purpose: to persuade a reader to do something — in this case, to award a higher mark. I recommend this practice. Rather than encouraging a deluge of disagreement which I initially feared, it encourages thoughtful reflection on the part of students, many of whom discover in the process of writing their challenge that the original assessment was a fair one. Those students who present convincing arguments for a higher mark earn it.

Collaborative Tests/Examinations

Because a growing number of teachers dislike traditional tests and examinations which conflict with the collaborative nature of their instruction, many have turned to tests and examinations that require cooperative effort by students and emphasize the learning process as well as the end result. While I discussed group interaction at length in Chapter 9, it is worthwhile noting here the possibilities this approach offers with regard to assessment.

Since I provide many opportunities for students to work together and to solve problems collaboratively, I cannot assess them fairly without offering assessment situations that allow them to work together. There are a number of vehicles teachers can use to accomplish this, but I have found it helpful to group them into two types: tests that require a single group response and those that allow individual students to confer with others in developing their responses to test items. Both require a positive climate of interdependence within a class, something which cannot be achieved without considerable planning and coaching on the part of the teacher and continued practice on the part of his students.

The first type involves a group of three to five students — who have already worked together on a number of occasions and are comfortable doing so — writing a test together. Depending on the scope of the test and the purpose of the assessment, I score the test in one of two ways, alerting my students in advance to the approach I will use:

1) I will select one test at random and mark only that one test, awarding the same value to all group members, or
2) I will assess all the tests, average the marks made by all group members, and award that average to each of them.

In both approaches, each member of the group is accountable to each of the others; not only must every group member try her best, she must make sure that all of her partners understand the task and try their best as well. Some students — and their parents — often resent this type of collaborative assessment because each person's mark is dependent upon the performance of other students which, in turn, is dependent as much upon interpersonal skills as upon the accomplishment of learning objectives. For these reasons, collaborative assessment comprises only a part of a student's overall mark, and I only assess students in this manner when I have taught them the interpersonal skills they require to function effectively in a group.

The second type of collaborative test also involves a group of three to five students who have already worked together on a number of occasions and are comfortable doing so. In this case, however, they are given the opportunity to collaborate on the task prior to producing a final response. In the case of a math test, for example, students might meet for several minutes to discuss a problem, clarifying what is asked, identifying the information that is needed, and sharing strategies for solving the problem. I have used this collaborative structure effectively in social studies and language arts assessment, too. For example, during a unit on short fiction with a senior English class, my students read a number of short stories and discussed the function of recurrent images and motifs and examined, as well, the importance of change in this genre, noting that most short stories include one of the following changes: 1) a change in the main character, or 2) a change in the main character's situation, or 3) a change in the reader's perception of the main character. It is these two ideas — image and change — which writers often use to convey a particular understanding about life and living that we call "theme."

In deciding how to assess my students' understanding of these concepts, I chose to involve them in the same process a short story writer would experience. I found a story I was sure my students would not have read, and I distributed copies lacking the final paragraph, which was the part of the story where the change is realized. The test would be comprised of two tasks: first, the students would "become" the writer and write these final lines, and then they would justify their ending in a short essay. Together we talked about the criteria that would determine a strong response. Obviously, I did not expect my students to invent the same ending the writer had penned; in fact, I told them I would assess only the essay that justified that ending. This led to a discussion of the elements that would demonstrate understanding of both writing style and the short story form: the use of a recurrent detail or motif, the inclusion of a change that grew naturally from the original story, and so on. My students had an evening to read the story and make notes in their reader's logs, and then I gave them the first period of a double class to discuss their ideas in small groups. During the second period, each student wrote her own ending — a handful of sentences — along with her justification of that ending. Not only did most individuals perform far better than I had hoped, they — and I — preferred many of the student endings to the writer's ending, which I later shared with them.

There are advantages to using collaborative assessment situations besides improved student performance. Students have the opportunity to use language to clarify and to generate meaning, something too often denied them in traditional settings. They see a direct benefit of working together as a community as opposed to working as isolated individuals, something which I want them to transfer to their lives beyond my classroom walls. Most important, though, collaborative tests promote learning as well as assess performance. How often can teachers claim that students actually learn while writing a test?

A Final Word about Tests: Learning from Them

While I have already talked about how teachers can learn from the tests they give students, I would also like to emphasize the importance of allowing students to learn from the tests they have written. From time to time when I return a math test, I offer students the opportunity to rewrite a test answer of their choice which they lost value on. However, they must do so in the following manner:

On a separate sheet of looseleaf which you will attach to your test paper, do the following:
1) identify the question you wish to do again,
2) explain in a few sentences where you went wrong in your original attempt,
3) do the question again, and
4) return your test to me by _____.

If students perform these tasks carefully, I reward them half the value they lost on their first attempt. In addition to allowing students to improve their scores, this opportunity is a mechanism by which they can improve their understanding of a concept or skill. Finally, it is a way I encourage my students to use language in their learning of math.

11 / Assessing Writing

Early in my teaching career, a group of teachers in the school where I was working asked me to join their writing group, which met every other Wednesday. Teaching five different courses, directing the school drama club, and coaching students for various public speaking competitions, I had little time to commit to another obligation. I almost declined the invitation, but I had enjoyed writing when I was younger and thought belonging to such a group might force me to make time for it again. It did. But it also did far more than that. It helped me recognize that the way I viewed writing as a teacher was far different than the way I viewed it when required to put words on paper for others to read.

In the days preceding each meeting, I struggled to find writing topics that interested me, scrapping dozens of attempts before settling on one I wanted to take further. I found pieces changing as I wrote them: letters became essays, short stories became poems, poems became kernels of longer pieces I had no idea how to write. Although the members of the group were colleagues and friends, I approached each meeting with a feeling beyond butterflies — two large California condors would suddenly take up residence in my stomach whenever it was my turn to share. And, although I could always depend on their responses being supportive and helpful, I agonized each time I waited for the others to comment. It was this opportunity to look at writing from the perspective of a writer that made me realize that the way I assessed student writing was not only unfair but counterproductive in terms of the learning I wanted my students to accomplish.

In my first few years in the classroom, I tried to assess everything my students wrote, the rationale being that if I didn't, they wouldn't think it important. With the possible exception of resentment — my students' — and physical exhaustion — my own — I accomplished very little. In trying to impress upon them the value of writing, I invariably showed them I didn't value theirs. In trying to help them see what writing could do *for* them, I showed them what it could do *to* them. Rather than seeing writing as a process, they viewed it as a recipe for a product few — if any — could create.

These experiences quickly showed me what educators like Karen Spear, Donald Murray, Nancie Atwell, Tom Romano, and others had learned long before:

1) students need opportunities to experiment in their writing without being penalized for it in subsequent assessment,
2) they need opportunities to "try out" their writing, to receive supportive feedback which will enable them to improve their pieces prior to assessment,
3) they need to have input into the selection of the pieces that will be assessed, and
4) they need a clear sense of the criteria the teacher will use to assess those pieces.

Many publications — including books by Spear, Murray, Atwell, and Romano — offer teachers excellent suggestions for providing students with these experiences. In this chapter, I will examine the fourth of these requirements: the criteria I use to assess students' writing.

What Is Good Writing?

Teachers are, to some degree, masochistic. I realized this recently as I reflected on the number of student writings I had read during my eighteen years in the classroom. I estimated the figure to be more than twelve thousand, not including tests and quizzes. It is unfortunate that I read the first two or three thousand of these clutching my red pen, vigorously participating in the ritual blood-letting I believed was a language art unto itself. Isn't that, I thought — if, indeed, I thought at all — what teachers do? Aren't we the keepers of the flame that is "good" writing?

It took some time for me to recognize that I brought to each piece I read the expectation that it would be "bad" writing.

Rather than focusing on what these writers had done well, I red-inked all their failures, reminding them that whatever they produced for me was less than it should be. What function — other than to justify the marks I assigned — did my red-inking serve? None I know of, since these pieces invariably went no further than the waste basket my students passed on their way out of my classroom.

I'm still doing penance for the pieces I responded to in this manner. And I'm grateful to the members of that writers' group who helped me recognize that every draft, no matter how hurried, contains something of value, some element worthy of positive response. There really is, after all my blood-letting, no such thing as "good" or "bad" writing. There is only writing that lies somewhere on the continuum between meaning approached and meaning made. As Peter Elbow explains, meaning isn't what the writer begins with; it's what she ends up with. It is the writer's commitment to discovering through the putting together of words on paper that determines the strength of her writing.

Fortunately, I've overcome my initial assumptions about student writing. Now I prefer to view a piece as either "strong" or "weak." Not only are these terms more descriptive of the potential of a piece of writing, they avoid the implication that good writing is produced by good people and bad writing by bad. What student, who for years has known that words are not his friends, needs to struggle with the added burden that his inability to use them stems from some character flaw?

Strong writing says what it wants to say. Although the writer may have coaxed it through several drafts, strong writing appears effortless. Strong writing elicits reader responses such as "Of *course!* That's *exactly* what I saw/heard/felt/tasted/smelled." "Hey! I've never *thought* of that." "I wish I'*d* written that." "How does this writer know me/my family/my life so well?" Weak writing, on the other hand, makes the reader aware of the writer's presence *above* the page, calls to mind an impression of one still in the process of choosing words and moving them around in search of the best possible order. Weak writing is meaning being approached. There is no blood in weak writing. There is flesh but no pulse.

What are the qualities that characterize strong writing? All teachers recognize that form and mechanics are important elements — the appearance of writing on the page and its observation of conventions of spelling, punctuation, and usage play a large part in ensuring that a piece says what it wants to say. However, writing can be technically accurate but lifeless; every word may be spelled correctly, every comma and period in the right place, but if the writer truly has nothing to say, no understanding he genuinely seeks to share with a reader, his piece becomes "Engfish," a term coined by one of Ken McCrorie's students and descriptive of much of the colourless writing submitted to teachers. While important, mechanics and form are surface features, the final considerations a writer makes when writing a piece. Engfish is avoided when writers first concern themselves with meaning.

In their excellent book *Inside Out: Developmental Strategies for Teaching Writing* (Boynton/Cook), Dan Kirby and Tom Liner suggest that strong writing has voice, movement, a light touch, and is both informative and inventive. Voice, they explain, is exactly what it suggests: the sense of one person talking to another. Writing that has voice leaves the reader with a strong impression of the person behind the pen, much like an impression left by an individual we have met for the first time and know in our hearts that we will want to meet again.

Movement involves the "building" of the piece, the sense that the writer is taking the reader someplace and knows how she will get there — the journey may be long or short, but there is a pattern to the process of discovery, a sense of order.

Writing reveals a light touch when the writer does not take herself too seriously. The writer may (indeed, should!) care passionately about her topic, but she does not allow this passion to cloud the fact that her reader may not feel the same, that her reader needs to be taken to the same place the writer has already arrived.

Informative writing is important, adding to the experience of the person reading. Writing that is inventive, explain Kirby and Liner, says something new, or says in a new way something that has been said before. Finding something new to write about can be difficult, even for the professional. Eudora Welty observed that few themes a person chooses to write about have not been written about before; however, it is the writer's unique vision of that theme which is important, which sets it apart, makes it worthwhile.

Strong writing reveals a sense of audience, anticipating a reader's need for information and understanding. Strong writing can only result when the writer has considered all his reader needs to know and has set about providing this information.

Strong writing is concrete and economical, using specific nouns and verbs to say in as few words as possible exactly what the writer means. Mark Twain wrote, "The difference between the right word and the nearly right word is the same as the difference between lightning and the lightning bug." Strong writing is filled with lightning.

Strong writing, continue Kirby and Liner, is rhythmic, using words that fit together with the natural cadence of human expression. Writers achieve this by reading aloud what they have written and listening to the sounds and the flow of their words. Robert Frost's definition of poetry as "the best possible words in the best possible order" may be applied to strong writing in general.

For me, writing is strong when it lifts me out of myself, makes a connection between me and another human being who has taken the time to use written language to share an experience or an understanding. Of course, students write more often for teachers because they *have* to than from a genuine desire, but even assigned writings can reflect the qualities Kirby and Liner have identified. When teachers recognize this, are able to see beyond the comma splices and dangling modifiers and the myriad surface concerns which occupy so much of the teaching and assessment of writing, they encourage students to see writing as more than an assigned task to be gutted by red pens — to see it as an opportunity to share in the discovery of meaning.

To accomplish this, I have prioritized the concerns I bring to writings which students submit for assessment.

Writing Priorities

Just as an apprentice carpenter doesn't learn how to trim a windowsill before he has learned how to build a sound structure that will hold the window, students need to be concerned about the "structure" of their pieces of writing before they become involved with the "trimmings," the matters of grammar and mechanics. These matters are important, but they are important in the *final* stages of writing — the editing and polishing of a piece which happens after the writer is satisfied he has said what he wants to say as clearly as he can. Drawing on the work of Nancie Atwell, Donald Murray, Peter Elbow, and other writing teachers, I adapted the following list of writing priorities — concerns about writing arranged in order of importance — which I consider when I respond to or assess a student's writing:

I. Content
   A. Purpose
      1. Has she made it clear what she wants her piece of writing to do?
      2. Has she made her purpose seem worthwhile?
      3. Does she show she has a particular audience in mind?
   B. Form
      1. Has he chosen a form that will do the job?
      2. Has he chosen a form that is appropriate for his audience?
   C. Information
      1. Has she said enough to get the job done?
      2. Do I need to know more?
   D. Focus
      1. Has he stayed on the topic without wandering?
      2. Has he included too much information that distracts me?

II. Arrangement of Ideas
   A. Order
      1. Are her ideas arranged in a definite order that is easy to follow?
      2. Does her piece have a definite beginning, middle, and end?
   B. Paragraphing
      1. Has he grouped together in paragraphs ideas that belong together?
      2. Has he paragraphed often enough to make his piece easy to read?
      3. Has he paragraphed too often, making it difficult for me to see connections in his writing?
   C. Transitions
      1. Has she used topic sentences or other clues to help me recognize her main points?

2. Has she used transitions to help connect one idea with the next, one part of her piece with the next?

III. Style
   A. Vividness
      1. Has he used strong verbs and nouns that say clearly what he means?
      2. Has he used examples and comparisons to show what he means?
      3. Has he used figurative language to create word pictures?
   B. Variety
      1. Has she chosen words carefully to avoid repetition?
      2. Has she used different types and lengths of sentences throughout?
      3. Has she included dialogue where possible?

IV. Editing Concerns
   A. Sentence problems: has he checked to make sure there are no
      1. sentence fragments?
      2. comma-splices?
      3. run-together sentences?
      4. wordy sentences?
      5. awkward sentences?
   B. Agreement problems: has she checked to make sure
      1. verb tense is the same throughout (unless flashbacks are used)?
      2. subjects and verbs agree in number?
      3. pronouns and antecedents agree in number?
      4. pronouns are the proper case?
   C. Mechanics: has he followed rules for
      1. capitalization?
      2. punctuation?
      3. spelling?
      4. usage?

Once I have made these priorities clear to my students, I develop rubrics suited to particular forms of writing — student-initiated as well as those I assign — which I will use when assessing student work. The advantages of rubrics were discussed in Chapter 7 along with examples of some I have used to assess specific writing assignments. A teacher may, however, prefer to develop a single rubric to use when assessing all writing tasks that are taken to a final, polished draft.

A Few Words about Courage

The single most important thing I keep in mind when assessing writing is that writing requires courage, regardless of the skill of the person holding the pen or tapping the keyboard. Winston Churchill described writing in these terms: "To begin with, it is a toy and an amusement. Then it becomes a mistress, then it becomes a master, then it becomes a tyrant." Although he was describing the writing of a novel, I think George Orwell captured most students' impressions of writing in general when he compared it to "a long bout of some painful illness. One would never undertake such a thing if one were not driven by some demon whom one can neither resist nor understand." Few students are demon-driven to put words on paper; most approach the task with the same sense of foreboding I experience each year I begin my income tax return. If I am to ensure that my assessment of their writing is both meaningful and accurate, I must acknowledge this fear and work to de-mystify the enigma students associate with the process of writing.

12 / Parents as Partners

My daughters love watching re-runs of the television program *Dinosaurs*. Their favourite character is the impish baby dinosaur who crows, "I'm the baby! Gotta love me!" The weeks before I began my first teaching assignment, I knew I would find it difficult developing a classroom management scheme that worked for me, and I realized there would be tough days ahead. However, when I thought about how I would interact with the parents of my students, I must have subconsciously believed, "I'm the teacher! Gotta love me!" I could not have been more wrong.

My first evening of parent-teacher interviews was a nightmare. Parents lined up outside my door in droves, and, as I attempted to justify to individual parents the reasons behind what I did in my classroom, I could hear three or four others in the hall complaining loudly about particular practices I'd adopted which they felt were not only unfair but ridiculous. I thought that evening would never end.

Some of the complaints were justified, arising from mistakes I had made due to my inexperience. (I can recall, for example, making one disruptive student stand with his nose against the blackboard simply because I had no idea what else to do to maintain control. Even now I shudder to think of it.) Most of the complaints, however, arose from practices — methodology-related as well as classroom management-oriented — which these parents simply did not understand. When I took the time to explain my reasons behind them, most were satisfied with my intentions and supportive of my efforts.

During that first year in the classroom, I made every mistake a teacher can possibly make and still remain employed. But I would not trade that year for anything because it taught me some important lessons that my Bachelor of Education training had not. One of the most important lessons I learned was that parents are not the enemy, that teachers who take the time to explain to parents the "why" and the "how" of what they do and maintain contact with parents throughout the school year have an enormous advantage over those teachers who do not do these things. In effect, these teachers are forging partnerships with parents that pay dividends in student achievement.

Communicating Expectations

As I explained in Chapter 5, I spend most of my first meeting with each class explaining what I expect of my students and what they can expect of me. I believe it is equally important to communicate this understanding to the parents of my students, and I use two methods to do this. The first is by letter, a copy of which goes home with each student the first day of school. The following is the letter I sent home this past September.

Dear Parents/Guardians:

I would like to take this opportunity to introduce myself and to let you know a little about what I expect of my students and what they can expect of me in the coming year. This is my eighteenth September as a teacher and, over the years, I have learned as much from my students as they have from me. One of the things they have taught me is that, in order for them to do the best they can, they require the following elements:

1) frequent communication between school and home,
2) knowledge of how to succeed,
3) organization, and
4) cooperation and encouragement of family members.

Regarding communication between school and home, this letter is an example of one of the ways I try to keep parents informed about what I am doing in my classroom. Also, during the year I try to phone or arrange meetings with parents when I feel they should be aware of certain developments, both positive and negative, in their son's/daughter's schooling. However, I want to encourage you to contact me whenever you have a question or a concern or a suggestion or simply a comment you would like to pass along. Either send in a note with your son/daughter or give me a call at the school or at my home. I appreciate hearing from parents because the more parents and teachers work together, the better we can expect students to do.

There is a saying that "Nothing succeeds like success." Without exception, students progress better in school when they experience success, and I believe students have a better chance of succeeding in a course when they know exactly what is required of them. Also, parents are better able to offer encouragement if they understand what is expected of their sons/daughters. Therefore, I have prepared a detailed course outline which includes the following information:

1) the objectives of the grade 8 math course,
2) a list of materials my students will need,
3) a description of what I require of my students each day,
4) an explanation of how I will assess my students, and
5) a description of the types of work they will do for me.

Please read this course outline and discuss it with your son/daughter. If you have any questions or concerns, please do not hesitate to contact me.

Also, I am attempting this year to offer an alternative program for students who have already mastered the skills associated with the regular grade 8 math program. The handout "MATH ENRICHMENT" explains how this alternative program will work. If you think your son/daughter would benefit from taking part in an enriched program, please read it over with him/her and answer the question at the bottom of that paper and send it back in. Again, if you have any questions (or suggestions), please give me a call.

The third element students require if they are to do well is organization. To help students get organized for math and keep themselves organized throughout the year, I have prepared a sheet called "ORGANIZING YOUR MATH BINDER" [see Appendix C] which I would like you to read. It would also be helpful if you would check your son's/daughter's math binder on a regular basis (for example, once each week) to see if he or she is following the instructions on this sheet.

Last, but certainly not least, is the role of the family in helping a student do well in school. I understand how difficult it is for parents to find time to help their sons/daughters with their schooling, especially with both parents working in so many families. (My wife and I both work, and we often find the task of parenting our two school-age children overwhelming.) However, I have prepared a list of simple suggestions titled

"HOW PARENTS CAN HELP" [included later in this chapter] which I would ask you to read and, again, discuss with your son/daughter.

I apologize for throwing so much information at you all at once, and I appreciate your efforts in wading through it. I would also appreciate it if you would complete the form below, then tear it off and send it in with your son/daughter as soon as possible.

Sincerely,

Don Aker
Teacher, Middleton Regional High School

(tear here)

NAME OF STUDENT: _____ CLASS: _____

I have read the "GRADE 8 MATH COURSE OUTLINE," the "ORGANIZ-ING YOUR MATH BINDER" handout, and the sheet titled "HOW PARENTS CAN HELP," and I have discussed them with my son/daughter.

_____   _____

(Signatures of parents/guardians)

_____

(Telephone number)

If you have any comments or questions or concerns, please feel free to write them below or on the back.

Along with this letter (and the other handouts noted above), I also send home a notice of a meeting I ask parents to attend, the second method I use to communicate my expectations. During the second week of school, I conduct a presentation during which I explain my program in more detail and answer any questions parents might have. One of the most important advantages afforded by this meeting is that it gives me an opportunity to meet parents even before I've got to know their sons and daughters. Not surprisingly, many adults feel uncomfortable entering a school, perhaps because some have unhappy memories of their own years as students. Meeting me like this at the very beginning of the school year allows them to get to know me as a person as well as a teacher; since I have no "history" with their sons or daughters, I am probably less threatening and more approachable than I might be if they met me for the first time in November during the regularly scheduled parent-teacher meetings.

Another important advantage this early meeting offers is the opportunity for parents to make suggestions about my program. During one summer, I spent considerable time designing an enrichment program for those students who could demonstrate prior proficiency in those areas I would be teaching. During my meeting with parents at the beginning of the new school year, I listened to several concerns about the enrichment program and entertained some interesting suggestions for ways to make it operate more equitably. While not all of these suggestions were feasible, one resulted in my making a major change regarding the post-test assessment of my partially-enriched students.

I cannot emphasize enough the importance of this initial contact with the families of the students I teach. Many of them have been actively involved in their children's elementary education, taking part in reading programs, school trips, presentations, and a host of other activities at this level. However, once their sons and daughters reach secondary school, opportunities for direct involvement are suddenly more limited. While there are secondary school teachers who emphasize parental and community involvement in their courses and classes, many do not and, as a result, parents suddenly find themselves seemingly cut off from their children's education. Therefore, with few exceptions, the parents of my students appreciate my efforts to explain my program in detail and to keep them informed of their sons' and daughters' progress. A direct result of my efforts is that these parents become my partners, continually reinforcing at home the very tenets I emphasize daily in my classroom.

Maintaining Contact with Parents

One of the criticisms leveled at secondary teachers is that their contact with parents is often minimal and is usually precipitated by something negative occurring in or outside the classroom. There are, obviously, reasons for this. At the elementary level where most teachers teach twenty-five to thirty-five students, maintaining regular contact is more manageable than at the secondary level where a teacher may teach more than 130 students. Depending on the programs they are teaching, some teachers meet in excess of 150 students every day. It is not surprising, therefore, that their contact with the home is limited to those times when there is a problem.

One way teachers can overcome this is to call the parents of at least two students each week solely for the purpose of passing along a positive comment. These calls need not be long — many last only three to four minutes — but they can have long-lasting results. Parents love being told when a son or daughter is performing well and, as a result, they become strong allies in the event the teacher has to call later about a problem. Students, as well, enjoy having their parents hear good things said about them and, as a result, they frequently perform better for those teachers who make such calls. Equally important is the support these parents can later lend to schools when criticism is leveled at teachers or programs. As various groups become more and more critical of education, a positive relationship between school and community is essential to the development of effective schools.

What can teachers say when they make these positive calls? While calls about superior academic performance are worthwhile, the teacher can also select a particular behaviour he would like to encourage. For example, when I see a student demonstrating strong leadership ability or being helpful to and supportive of other students, I make a note to call parents and tell them about it. After I make this call, I can be sure to see the student continuing to practice such behaviours and I sometimes see other students begin to do the same.

Besides this positive contact with the home, teachers should strive to keep parents abreast of students' academic performance — strong or weak. It is common for schools to have four reporting periods during the year, but these often fall into the "too little, too late" category. Parents appreciate being informed more frequently of their son's/daughter's performance so they can take measures to help them improve if problems exist. It does them little good to learn of a student's failing performance when it is too late to help him improve sufficiently to pass or, more important, to achieve the learning objectives that are prerequisite to his later success.

Regardless of the reason for the contact, I find it helpful to keep records of calls to parents. In my record binder, I record the date and time and reason for the contact, the person I spoke to, and the result of the conversation. Also, I make a note of any follow-up action I might need to take; for example, in cases where I phone parents about students who are not doing homework, they often ask me to call again in a couple of weeks to tell them whether their son or daughter has improved in this area. I also add this to my calendar so I do not forget. If I tell a parent I am going to do something but I do not follow through on it, I lose credibility not only with the parent but with the student as well.

Reporting Academic Performance

I noted in Chapter 1 that one of the problems with the report cards issued by secondary schools is that they often have little more than a percentage recorded beside a student's name. Parents — and, more important, the students themselves — usually have little idea how that percentage was calculated and, therefore, are unable to celebrate individual successes or to identify specific weaknesses that need to be addressed. Therefore, I believe it is my job to make sure my students — and their parents — understand how I arrive at their marks; to do this, I prepare a report for each student that breaks down the mark according to each assessment component.

Parents are very appreciative of this breakdown of assessment scores, especially when it identifies specific areas a student was not performing well in which they can encourage that student to work toward improving. However, the time required to prepare these assessment breakdowns is considerable, and I welcome the advent of computer software, which now makes this task far less arduous. For example, my school uses Integrade, a program that not only calculates report marks from scores I enter but also features an option which allows me to print out a spreadsheet for every student that is very task-specific. Besides listing every task entered, the value it was marked out of, and the score the student received on each, it also converts each score to a percentage, identifies the value of the task in relation to the total report mark, and lists the average mark scored by the entire class on each task along with the standard deviation. The real benefit of using the Integrade program is that two simple keystrokes enable me to print off a detailed, up-to-date spreadsheet for any student at any time, provided I have entered all my marks.

I have students take spreadsheets home to be signed and returned; I then file them in a folder which I can refer to easily. These signed spreadsheets are not only excellent evidence of student achievement but also a record of my having kept both students and their parents informed of their progress.

Reporting Assessment of Specific Tasks

Although the computer spreadsheet is an excellent device for reporting information about student performance, teachers should not overlook the importance of immediately conveying assessment information about specific tasks. For example, when I return to students an assignment or a test that represents a major part of their assessment in my course, I require that they get their parents to sign them. (If, by the way, I am suspicious about the authenticity of a signature, I check the sheet I had students get signed the first day of school — I keep these on file.) In signing tests and projects, parents are able to share in the student's success as well as read specific comments I may have made which alert them to weaknesses the student needs to address. Often, parents will contact me by note or by phone as a result of a student's performance on a particular task. The advantage of this is that the mark a student eventually receives at the end of a reporting term is a surprise to no one.

The only tasks I do not allow students to keep are their mid-year and final examinations, although they are able to see their mid-year exam in the class following the examination period. However, I feel it is extremely important to convey to parents information about this task, so I send home a breakdown of each student's performance on the exam. In this way, the student and her parents can identify specific areas which need to be addressed to ensure future success in my course as well as successive programs. Below is the breakdown I gave to my academic students when I returned their Christmas examination this year. (Students working on modified programs wrote a different examination and received a different breakdown specific to their exam.) After we looked at the examination as a whole, I asked them to complete the form by filling in the scores they had made on each question.

114

The following is a breakdown of the Christmas exam according to the type of questions asked. Fill in the scores you made on each question to determine what areas (if any) you need to concentrate on improving.

SECTION A:
This section tested your knowledge of the language of math (the words we use when we say numbers, describe operations, etc.).

#1 __   #2 __   #3__   #4__   #5__   = __
  3   2   4   3   1   13 (Total for
                                                      SECTION A)

SECTION B:
This section tested your number knowledge such as place value, expanded forms, symbols such as < and >, etc.

#6 __   #7 __   #8 __   #9 __   #10__   = __
  2   3   1   3   4   13 (Total for
                                                      SECTION B)

SECTION C:
This section tested your understanding of the rules for the order of operations as well as your ability to perform calculations.

#11__   #12__   = __
  10   3   13 (Total for
                                                      SECTION C)

And so on.

Conducting a Parent-Teacher Interview

As I wrote earlier in this chapter, parents are not the enemy. However, it can sometimes seem that way when parents approach us with concerns about what and how we are teaching their sons and daughters. The important thing to remember is that parents often hear only one side of an issue — the student's — and we must be willing and able to clarify misunderstandings without becoming defensive. For example, this year I received a phone call from a mother who was concerned with an instruction I had given her son prior to the first test of the year. "Sandy," she insisted, "said you told his class they shouldn't study the night before a test." What I had actually told Sandy's class was that students should not be studying anything *new* the night before a test; they should be *reviewing* the material they have already studied in the days prior to the test. In other words, students should not cram — instead, they should make a study schedule and stick to it. When I explained this to Sandy's mother, she understood my instruction and was more than willing to help Sandy prepare for my tests in this manner.

From time to time, despite a teacher's efforts to establish contact with the home and convey information about course objectives and student performance, friction can occur between the teacher and the student's family. Early in my career, for example, I taught a student who disliked me from the moment he stepped into my classroom, and his parents shared his feeling toward me. Being inexperienced, I felt threatened and intimidated each time they asked to meet with me. As I became more accustomed to such meetings, however, I was able to identify strategies to help make these meetings less confrontational and more productive:

1) Remember that, first and foremost, the parents are concerned for their son or daughter — if they weren't, they would not be there. What may appear to be a personal vendetta against you is really an attempt to do what is best for the student. If you keep this in mind, it will help focus attention on the problem and lead to a solution.

2) Bear in mind that some parents react negatively toward teachers because of their own negative experiences with school. Try to put the parents at ease by shaking hands and commenting first on a safe topic; even simple remarks about the weather can help set the tone for a productive meeting. Arrange to have the meeting in a neutral area; rather than in the principal's office or your classroom, conduct the meeting in the guidance department or library or other comfortable area when it will be free of interruptions.

3) Ask an administrator to be present at these meetings. She will be able to act as a mediator should agreement be difficult to reach. Also, her presence will help ensure that discussion is non-confrontational.

4) Decide in advance whether the student should be present

at such a meeting. Initial meetings are often less threatening for a teacher if the student is not present; however, much can be accomplished by having the student there to respond to particular concerns addressed by both her teacher and her parents.

5) Know in advance what you want to say. It's always a good idea to jot down important points so you won't forget them. Also, find out from other teachers how the student is performing for them — this information may provide you with further insight into the nature of the problem.

6) Establish a timeframe for the meeting. Meetings tend to be more productive when participants know when they must end.

7) Identify at the beginning of the meeting what those present are trying to accomplish. The student should be the focus of the group's efforts — the purpose of the meeting should be stated in terms of how it will benefit the student.

8) Ask to hear the parents' concerns first. Listen attentively to what they have to say, watching their faces as they speak and nodding to indicate agreement where possible.

9) Be prepared with records and examples of the student's performance. Even during routine parent-teacher interviews, for example, I organize copies of spreadsheets, examinations, portfolios, and records of student performance, as well as copies of relevant materials such as the course outline. Teachers who have to dig through piles of files to find information do not present themselves in a positive light.

10) Be prepared with a record of your past efforts to address any problem you are having with the student. Provide a list of dates and times you met with the student as well as dates and times you contacted the home.

11) Conduct yourself professionally. Should a meeting become confrontational, keep a cool head. Calmly but firmly insist on civility and model this conduct yourself. If tempers flare, suggest the meeting be rescheduled for a time when discussion will be more productive. Never allow a meeting to deteriorate into a shouting match.

12) At the end of the meeting, review the purpose of the meeting and have each member present state what he or she will do to help improve the situation. If necessary, draw

up a timeline to ensure completion of particular tasks. No one should be unclear about subsequent responsibilities.

13) Before the meeting ends, be sure to thank the parents for their interest. Their time is valuable, too, and their willingness to meet with you should be appreciated.

14) Keep the parents informed about the situation and report any developments, positive as well as negative, by phone or by note.

Suggestions to Offer Parents

Few problems, of course, can be solved with a single meeting. The important thing to remember is that, together, parents and teachers can accomplish much more than they can working independently of each other. The greater the communication between home and school, the greater the likelihood students will achieve success.

For those students who experience particular difficulty in the courses I teach, I offer parents the following suggestions:

1) Insist on seeing your son's/daughter's work on a regular basis — every day to begin with, then periodically to check on his/her performance. Contact me if you have particular concerns.

2) Require your son/daughter to carry a notebook which I will use to communicate information regarding assignments, tests, classroom performance, etc. For example, at the end of each period, the student should write out the assignment and bring it to me to be signed, at which point I can, if necessary, make a quick comment about his/her performance. If the notebook comes home unsigned, you are to phone me at home that evening for information regarding his/her assigned work.

3) Call me at school or at home (between 6:30 and 7:30 on school nights) on a regular basis (for example, once every two weeks) to find out how your son/daughter is performing. I always keep my record of student performance handy so I can identify at a glance any tasks a student has not completed and any behaviours that need to be reinforced.

While some teachers may not wish to have parents call them at home, I find this one of the most effective means of keeping parents informed and keeping students on track. Most calls take only a few minutes, and parents appreciate teachers who make themselves accessible. Those teachers who prefer not to be called at home can arrange to be available at the school at a regular time each day.

One of the comments I hear most often from parents is, "I want to help, but I don't know what I can do." When students move from elementary to secondary schools, they also begin a journey that takes them away from their parents. They want more freedom, fewer restrictions, and, ultimately, more control over their lives. While this is a time when parents must redefine limitations and reassess expectations, it is not a time to abdicate their authority. More than any other time in their sons' and daughters' lives, they need to maintain a strong presence. To assist the parents of my junior-high students in maintaining this presence, I send home the following suggestions at the beginning of the year and address many of them during our first meeting in September. While they are aimed at parents of junior-high students, these suggestions can be adapted to assist parents of older students.

HOW PARENTS CAN HELP

One important part of being a parent is helping your son/daughter develop good study habits. Below are ten simple suggestions I would like to offer, which, I am sure, most parents are already doing:

1) Make sure your son/daughter attends school. Except in cases of illness or family emergency, students should not miss classes.
2) Set aside a regular time every school night when your son/ daughter will work on schoolwork. Even if he/she has no written homework (which will seldom happen), he/she should spend the time reviewing what has been done in class and looking ahead to see what is coming.
   NOTE: This time should be free of ALL distractions including music, television, telephone, etc. Some students feel they can study better in front of the TV or with music in the background, but this is simply not true. Also, they should not be interrupted by family members during this time. If there are chores to be done, they should be done before or after this study time. Finally, take telephone messages or ask callers to phone back rather than letting phone calls interrupt study time.
3) Provide a place where your son/daughter can work that has plenty of light, room, and materials to get the job done (pens, pencils,

paper, reference books, etc.). It might be in a separate room or simply at the kitchen table, but it should not be near a window or near a lot of activity that will distract him/her.

4) Make sure your son/daughter knows HOW to study. Some students think that studying is simply reading the material, but this is *not* an effective way to study. I will offer suggestions to my students for the best ways to study math, but the school guidance department also has plenty of information on study skills which students or their parents can have if they request it.

5) Keep a calendar posted in the kitchen with all upcoming events and assignments on it. Include family and social events as well as tests/projects/etc. because these are all things that require time. If the whole family knows what things are coming up, it will be easier to remember them and plan time for them.

6) Talk to your son/daughter about school. Ask questions about what he or she is doing in his/her classes. Don't be satisfied with an answer like "Nothing." The more interest you show in what he/she is doing, the more likely it is that he/she will try to do well *and* will come to you when there is a problem.

7) Frequently ask to see your son's/daughter's work and praise him/her for work done well. If you think there is room for improvement, encourage him/her to do better. (It is generally *not* a good idea to offer rewards such as money or gifts for doing well in school. Encouragement and praise are better motivators.)

8) Contact teachers from time to time to find out how your son/daughter is doing. Most teachers will call you if there is a problem, but if *you* call teachers periodically, this will also show your son/daughter that you are interested in how he/she is doing. It will also show his/her teachers that you are interested in your son's/daughter's learning and are willing to help.

9) Make sure your son/daughter gets plenty of rest. No student can do his/her best if he/she stays up too late. Agree on a regular "lights out" time.

10) Encourage your son/daughter to read for pleasure. All too often, students tend to turn on the TV for entertainment, but reading more can improve a student's performance in school. The local library has (or can get) nearly any book a student might like to read. If possible, make time for the whole family to go sign out books. Ask your son/daughter to tell you about what he/she is reading, and talk to him/her about what you are reading.

On Forming the Partnership

Without question, the family is an institution that has undergone radical change in the last few decades. Single-parent as well as blended families are now the norm in many communities, and few families have a parent who remains in the home every day. Despite these changes, however, the family still plays a major role in the success of students at the secondary level, and most parents welcome practical strategies for effectively supporting their sons'/daughters' learning. The time a teacher spends communicating with parents will be reflected not only in improved student performance but also in strong ties with the community. As schools move toward more site-based and community-oriented designs, these ties will be invaluable components of successful and effective teaching.

Afterword

"This is quite possibly the last barbecue cover you'll ever buy."

That comment was printed on the package containing a vinyl cover I bought for our gas barbecue last year. Actually, I end up buying a cover almost every year because our barbecue remains outside on our deck — even in winter — and, by the time spring rolls around, the cheap cover I usually buy for it has begun to look like the victim of a wayward airplane propeller. So last year I splurged and purchased the most expensive cover I could find. Already, however, I'm beginning to suspect that it won't be the last one I'll ever buy.

Nor will this book be the last on assessment you will ever read. And it shouldn't be. If there is one thing I have learned about education that is a constant, it is the fact that there are few constants in education. Our profession is continually in flux, continually re-examining itself, seeking better ways of meeting the needs of the students who enter our schools and our classrooms every year. My approach to assessment is one that has evolved over all the years I have been in the classroom and is far different than the approach I used at the beginning of my career. And it will continue to evolve as my students teach me more about how they learn and what I need to look for to understand how they learn. I don't believe a teacher ever gets to the point where she feels she has all the answers. If this happens, I suspect she may have stopped asking questions. As teachers, we must always ask those questions and be willing to share with others the answers we discover. Keep asking your own questions. And keep sharing the answers you discover.

Regardless of what Polonius said, we can be borrowers *and* lenders.

Appendix A

STUDENT:_____ CLASS:_____ DATE:_____

Dear Parent/Guardian,

This is to inform you that _____ disrupted my class today with behaviour that was not appropriate. Please sign below indicating that you are aware of his/her actions, and please encourage him/her to remember what is expected in my classroom.

Sincerely,
Don Aker

_____
(Signature of parent/guardian)

Appendix B

Dear Parents/Guardians:

During the years I have been a classroom teacher, I have learned as much from my students as they have from me, and one of the most important lessons they have taught me is that they learn best in a classroom that runs smoothly. To make sure that my classroom runs efficiently and that my students are treated as fairly as possible, I ask them to follow five rules:

1) Bring to class the books and materials needed.
2) Settle down to work as quickly as possible.
3) Raise your hand if you wish to speak.
4) Respect the needs and feelings of others.
5) Plan to learn, and plan to help others learn.

To ensure that these rules are followed, I let my students know when they are creating problems. If a student behaves in a way that I find disruptive, I write his or her name on the board. I make no comment and continue with the lesson — the name on the board is simply a signal to this student that he or she has been warned. If the student stops being disruptive, no further action is taken. If, however, the student continues to be disruptive, I put a checkmark beside his or her name. If the disruptive behaviour continues, more checkmarks are added. The following is an explanation of the consequences of these checkmarks:

  ✓ The student is given a note to take home explaining that he/she has been disruptive; a parent or guardian must sign the note and the student must bring it to class the next day. The student may not be allowed to return to class until the signed note is returned.

✓ On the *following* school day at 12:35, the student must come to my classroom and spend fifteen minutes in detention. The student may not be allowed to return to my class until the detention has been served.

✓✓✓ On the *following* school day at 12:35, the student must come to my classroom and spend thirty minutes in detention. The student may not be allowed to return to my class until the detention has been served.

✓✓✓✓ The student is sent to the Vice-Principal's office where further action will be taken.

Please note that these checkmarks are not carried over from one day to the next — every student starts with a clean slate each day. I would like to point out that in all the years I have used this system, no student has received four checkmarks. Most students respond well to the warning (the name on the board), and only a few have received two or three checkmarks.

It would be a great help to me if you and your son or daughter would please sign below indicating that you have read the procedure outlined above. If you have any questions or concerns, please call me at school or at my home. Also, please feel free to contact me throughout the year if you would like to talk about your child's progress. I appreciate hearing from parents.

Sincerely,
Don Aker
Teacher, Middleton Regional High School

_____   _____
(Student's signature)   (Signature of parent/guardian)

                               _____
                               (Signature of parent/guardian)

Appendix C

ORGANIZING YOUR MATH BINDER

Whether it be in school or at a job or even when taking a vacation, a person's success usually depends on how well organized he or she is. The following instructions will help you organize your math binder, and I will check it occasionally to make sure you are keeping it organized all year long.

1) On the inside front cover of your math binder, tape a copy of your timetable AND a mini-calendar which shows the months from September to June.

2) Place your course outline *and* this handout at the beginning of your binder so you can find them easily if you need to refer to them.

3) Using dividers, separate your binder into the following sections: VOCABULARY, PROBLEM-SOLVING STRATEGIES, QUIZZES, TESTS, PROJECTS, UNIT 1, UNIT 2, UNIT 3, UNIT 4, UNIT 5, UNIT 6, UNIT 7, UNIT 8, UNIT 9, and UNIT 10.

4) At the back of your binder, keep *plenty* of lined looseleaf and a few sheets of unlined looseleaf and graph paper.

5) At the beginning of each class, begin a new sheet of looseleaf.

6) Write the date on the top line on your looseleaf at the *right*.

7) Copy the lesson number (for example, "Lesson 7") on the top line of your looseleaf at the *left*.

8) On the second line, write the word OBJECTIVES and, after it, copy the objectives I will give you. For example, the objective of lesson 7 is, "Calculate number expressions using the rules for the order of operations."

9) If I give you a handout, date it in the upper right corner and place it in your binder after the sheet of looseleaf

having the same date.

10) When I give you an assignment, write it down clearly (along with the date it is due) in your homework notebook. Do not leave the classroom until you are sure you understand what you have to do.

11) Homework assignments should be done on looseleaf following the work done in class. At the beginning of each homework assignment, write HOMEWORK and the date the assignment was given. When you are doing an assignment from the textbook, write the page number of the textbook above the assignment and underline it (for example, PAGE 23). Then write the question number in the left margin beside each question. ALWAYS BEGIN A QUESTION AT THE MARGIN.

12) When doing a math question, do the following:
   a) Work *neatly* in pencil.
   b) Show all work. Even if you use a calculator, show the operations used to find the answers.
   c) Write your answers in complete statements when questions are asked or problems are given. For example, *The average price is $20.00.*
   d) If you are asked to draw a chart or graph, give it a title. For example, "Population of Middleton Regional High School."
   e) Leave white space around each problem and *underline* your final answer to long calculations.

13) If you discover you have done a question wrong, draw a circle around it and write WRONG beside the circle. Then, include the correct answer AND the procedure beside it.

14) When I ask you to write a test or quiz, write TEST or QUIZ at the top of your looseleaf along with your name and the date in the upper right corner.

15) When I return a quiz, place it in the "QUIZZES" section of your binder in order according to the date. If you have done something wrong, follow the instructions given in #13.

16) When I return a test, place it in the "TESTS" section of your binder in order according to the date. If you have done something wrong, follow the instructions given in #13.

* * * * * * * * * * *

Appendix D

The following books are excellent resources for teachers interested in learning about group process.

Atwell, Nancie (1987). *In the Middle: Writing, Reading, and Learning with Adolescents*. Upper Montclair, NJ: Boyton/Cook Publishers, Inc.

Clarke, Judy, and Wideman, Ron, and Eadie, Susan (1990). *Together We Learn*. Scarborough, ON: Prentice-Hall.

Hill, Susan, and Hill, Tim (1990). *The Collaborative Classroom: A Guide to Co-operative Learning*. Portsmouth, NH: Heinemann.

Schmuck, Richard A., and Schmuck, Patricia A. (1988). *Group Processes in the Classroom*. Dubuque, IA: William C. Brown.

Slavin, Robert E. (1983). *Cooperative Learning*. New York, NY: Longman.

Spear, Karen (1988). *Sharing Writing: Peer Response Groups in English Classes*. Portsmouth, NH: Heinemann.

Spear, Karen, et al (1993). *Peer Response Groups in Action: Writing Together in Secondary Schools*. Portsmouth, NH: Heinemann.

4722